BANG OUT OF ORDER!

The Rise and Fall of
Actor Derek Newark

PETER NEWARK

BROWN
DOG
BOOKS

Copyright © Peter Newark 2016

The right of Peter Newark to be identified as the author of this work has been asserted in accordance with the Copyright, Designs and Patents Act 1988.

All rights reserved. No part of this book may be reproduced, stored in a retrieval system, or transmitted in any form or by any means, electronic, electrostatic, magnetic tape, mechanical, photocopying, recording or otherwise without the written permission of the copyright holder, except by a reviewer who wishes to quote brief passages in connection with a review written for insertion in a magazine, newspaper or broadcast.

Published under licence by Brown Dog Books and the Self-Publishing Partnership,
7 Green Park Station, Bath BA1 1JB.
www.selfpublishingpartnership.co.uk

All photographs from the Derek Newark Private Collection.

The author has made every effort to clear all copyright permissions, but where this has not been possible and amendments are required, the author will be pleased to make any necessary arrangements at the earliest opportunity.

ISBN printed book: 978-1-78545-091-4
ISBN e-book: 978-1-78545-092-1

Cover design by Kevin Rylands
Internal design by Andrew Easton

Printed and bound by CPI Group (UK) Ltd, Croydon CR0 4YY

Contents

	Acknowledgements	7
1	A Night Out with John Bindon	9
2	The Boy with the Golden Voice	19
3	An Officer and a Comedian	30
4	Training at RADA	47
5	Nearly Drowned by Michael Winner	56
6	Brecht and Boozing	78
7	'I don't mind type-casting'	95
8	A National Disaster	109
9	A Bedroom on Broadway	138
10	Best Ever Performance	148
11	Worst Ever Performance	176
12	The Soho Scene	195
13	'Do you want to fight me?'	210
14	The Final Curtain	231
	Index	249

*This book is dedicated to all the actors,
writers, directors, and backstage staff of the
bygone Cottesloe Theatre Company, that
trail-blazing troupe of pioneers that made
stage history at the Royal National Theatre.*

Acknowledgements

I wish to express my thanks to the following people and institutions for their help and assistance towards the making of this book. Firstly, the entire Newark family for their separate contributions, and in particular my son Tim who edited the manuscript and supervised the book production.

I am grateful to the following for providing information and anecdotes: Nigel Arthur, curator of BFI Archive; Ashley Brown, publisher; Brian Cox, actor; Kenneth Cranham, actor; Michael Dillon of Gerry's Club; Tony Haygarth, actor; Martin Jarvis, actor; Colonel Brian Kay; Erin Lee, National Theatre Studio; Emily Morris, National Theatre Archive; RADA Archive. I would also like to acknowledge with thanks the following authors whose work has proved invaluable: Jack Shepherd and Keith Dewhurst, *Impossible Plays: Adventures with the Cottesloe Company* (Methuen Drama, 2006), and Daniel Rosenthal, *The National Theatre Story* (Oberon Books, 2013). Thanks also to Punch Ltd for permission to publish the Hewison cartoon.

And not forgetting all those fellow actors and theatre folk who worked and drank with Derek Newark over the years and have passed away to join him in that Green Room in the sky. I thank you one and all.

Peter Newark, 2016

BANG OUT OF ORDER!

CHAPTER 1
A Night Out with John Bindon

Derek needed a drink. He had just completed another intense evening's performance starring as the enigmatic Colonel Roote in Harold Pinter's perplexing play, *The Hothouse*, to a mystified and lukewarm audience. The time: late April 1980. The place: Derek's dressing room at the Hampstead Theatre in London's Swiss Cottage Centre.

'I need a bloody drink,' he said to a cast member. 'A poor house tonight. They didn't get the play at all... I sometimes feel I'm wasting my bloody time.'

His adrenalin was still pumping. He wanted a drink, but not just a quick shot of vodka. His hungry ego craved attention. He wanted to drink in convivial company, in acquiescent company, with people who valued his worth, who admired his acting ability. When his colleague mentioned a party in progress in a Chelsea club, Derek was keen to join him.

At the lively venue, Derek soon attracted a small group of admirers and he entertained them with his usual stock of show business anecdotes, embellished with his clever mimicry; he did a very funny John Gielgud. Derek was in his element, the centre of attention. He then spotted the formidable figure of 'Big John'

BANG OUT OF ORDER!

Bindon across the room, sitting on a sofa with his brawny arms draped over the shoulders of a pair of giggling girls.

Bindon clocked Derek standing at the bar. They exchanged nods of recognition. Bindon was a small-part actor in TV and films. Derek knew him slightly, having worked in the same TV series, *Z-Cars* and *Department S*, but he had little regard for Bindon's acting ability.

'He's not much of a player,' he said to me. 'He's one-dimensional. A one-trick pony—Cockney hard bastard. There's nothing else in the man.'

But Derek was not entirely correct. Bindon was not just a jobbing actor of little talent. He had another line of enterprise: he was also a real-life notorious villain, an associate of the infamous Kray Twins and other leading criminals. He presented an impressive physique: six feet two in height, with a bull-neck, and powerful butcher's hands ridged with prominent misshapen knuckles. He was solidly built like a tank, or, as Derek so elegantly put it, 'like a brick shithouse'. He possessed great strength, was maniacally fearless, without mercy and without normal conscience.

Indeed, there was nothing normal about 'Big John' Bindon. It was well known that he possessed an abnormally large penis that he would proudly display to both genders in private and public places. He had a string of female lovers. In short, he was a crude and cruel brute of a man. Raised in a rough working-class area of London, he had known violence all his life, and he enjoyed inflicting harm on others. Gangland employed him as an 'enforcer' to gather outstanding debts and to punish rivals.

Derek was well aware of Bindon's nefarious reputation. A

BANG OUT OF ORDER!

year earlier he had been acquitted at a murder trial of stabbing a gangster to death in a club. Bindon, having suffered severe wounds in the knife-fight, pleaded self-defence. Bob Hoskins, the popular Cockney actor, appeared as a character witness for Bindon. Asked to explain the defendant's nickname of 'Biffo', Hoskins said it referred to the comic creation 'Biffo the Bear', and not to Bindon's propensity for punching people. To much surprise, 'Biffo' walked free. The back-story is a complex one but the fact remains that Bindon got away with murder.

After that, his acting career faded away and he relied even more on his underworld activities for an income. Being a known killer gave him kudos in the social crowd in Chelsea and Fulham. People who should have known better embraced his notoriety. His very presence exuded an aura of violence. Not a man to trifle with, a word out of place brought a fist to the face. It was known that he carried a knife tucked into a cowboy boot.

Now this monster was staring hard at Derek across the crowded room, making him feel very uncomfortable. Then Bindon got up and swaggered over to an anxious Derek. He extended a butcher's hand in friendship.

'Hello Derek, nice to see you,' he said with a cold-eyed smile. 'Must say you're doing very well these days.'

Derek grinned back and modestly shrugged off the compliment.

'Saw you in that *Hothouse* the other night,' Bindon continued. 'What a lot of codswallop that was. Didn't know what was going on... walked out half-way through.'

Derek was now faced with a cultural dilemma. What to say to a dangerous, hair-triggered ignoramus? One wrong word and Biffo...

'Yes, I somewhat agree,' said a cautious Derek. 'It's a very difficult play to understand...'

Bindon cut him short.

'Nah, don't get me wrong, Derek, I thought you was great, a great performance. You was the main man. I admire proper actors like you, trained actors who speak properly, with a wide range, know what I mean. Take me, I was dead lucky, I got away with murder...'

Derek interrupted with 'Yes, the trial must've been an ordeal...'

Bindon cut him short again.

'Nah, not that spot of bleeding bother, I mean I got away with murder in the acting game. Couldn't believe my luck. It was all a lark to me.'

Bindon was ten years younger than Derek, born in 1943. At the age of 23, he was spotted by chance in a pub by the film director Ken Loach who cast him as Tom, the brutal wife-beater of Carol White in the grim working-class docudrama *Poor Cow*, released in 1967. It launched Bindon's short acting career. He appeared on TV and in a few movies in the same typecast roles as crooks, cops, and various hard men. But he was a severely limited player and proved difficult to work with. When the acting jobs dried-up, he concentrated on his criminal career.

'Do you like this club?' Bindon asked Derek, who was now relieved and somewhat relaxed at the friendly meeting.

'Yes, nice place,' he replied.

'Yeah, nice and quiet,' said Bindon. 'No trouble, no bother, know what I mean? I'm in the club business now. Got an interest in this gaff, and some others.'

In fact, he was in the protection racket. Nightclubs were,

and are, lucrative but vulnerable to gang violence. Bindon, the lone 'protector', collected regular 'insurance' fees from club owners in return for keeping the club safe from other invading gangsters who might wreck the place. A case of paying the poacher to ward off other poachers.

'Yeah, I think you're a diamond actor, Derek,' the amiable Bindon continued. 'You was very funny in *Bedroom Farce.*'

By now, sipping yet another vodka, the conceited Derek was savouring all the flattery that Big John dished up.

'I wish I could be like you,' said the seemingly obsequious Bindon. 'Do what you do—sad stuff, comic stuff, Shakespeare stuff.'

Derek was now in patronising mode.

'My dear chap, if only you'd had the training, I'm sure you would...'

Bindon interrupted: 'Know what, Derek, I'd like to be your friend, a good mate. Let me give you a little tour of my clubs.'

Derek found it difficult to refuse such a cordial offer and he agreed to the tour. And off they went into the night, the actor with his new-found friend, the hardest bastard in London.

Almost a matched pair in appearance, Derek was 47 years old, six feet tall, burly, hard of face when not smiling, still fit and strong. He looked the part of a villain. After calling at several clubs where they were treated like VIPs, with drinks on the house, Bindon decided to visit a new club recently opened. The two bouncers on the door greeted Bindon with due respect.

'Evening, John. No bother, yeah?'

'Nah,' said Bindon, 'no bother, just wanna quick drink.'

The room was full of well-dressed men and girls, with an element of tough-looking geezers. Bindon ordered the barman

BANG OUT OF ORDER!

to run a tab, meaning keep the drinks coming and I'll pay later. Standing at the bar, Derek was talking to one chap, and Bindon was chatting to another guy. Suddenly, the convivial situation was shattered when Big John shouted in anger: 'You taking the piss!' And punched the man he had been talking to, sending him crashing into a table full of drinks and guests.

Bindon then commenced punching all unfortunate men within range. Women screamed in terror. The bouncers came running. Big John commanded them to 'stay outta this or I'll kill you!' Bindon in roaring Viking berserker mode was indeed a daunting sight, and the bouncers sought refuge at the door. Meanwhile, Derek had become immediately embroiled in the fracas when a tough geezer threw a punch and he retaliated... and was soon fighting for survival. After several violent minutes, Bindon grabbed Derek's arm.

'Let's get outta here!' and they ran for the door, leaving the place in a shambles.

On the way out, Bindon gave one of the bouncers a wad of bank notes, saying: 'This is for you. Tell your boss I'll be back to talk business.'

Out in the cool night air, Bindon put some more notes into the top pocket of Derek's ripped jacket, telling him, 'Get a cab, Derek, you done well.'

And they went their separate ways. Derek still shaken by the unexpected affray
A few days later, on hearing the gossip going the rounds about Bindon's 'gang' being involved in another escapade (nothing appeared in the newspapers; no complaints had been made to the police), Derek fully realised that he had been manipulated

into the night club fight.

'That cunning bastard conned me into that punch-up. He used me and I fell for it. He was bang out of order.'

Big John had indeed fooled Derek with a lot of well-planned flattery into giving him muscle support in the tricked-up fracas that enabled him to add yet another club to his protection racket. Derek, nursing his bruised ego, stayed well clear of the man thereafter. His final sagacious comment on the episode: 'It seems that Bindon is a far better actor than I gave him credit for.'

*****

Derek Newark was not a national, nor an international star of wide public fame. He was not, in show business parlance, a marquee name. He was, however, a very familiar face on British television for thirty years. He was a solid, positive supporting actor to many stars of theatre and cinema. He sparkled up there on stage and screen with most of the prominent British actors of his time. He appeared on Broadway in a smash-hit comedy. He exchanged party banter with the playwright Tennessee Williams, and discussed the plays of Arthur Miller with... Miller himself. He dined with James Mason, who found him an amusing companion. He played poker with the Hollywood film star George Peppard, and lost, then played him at squash, and won, much to the chagrin of the narcissistic 'Perfect George'. And while waiting around on film sets, Derek enjoyed trading bitchy gossip with the elegant John Gielgud (who told him a most outrageous story!).

In his time, Derek trod the boards with a veritable host of top-rated talent. He worked at his craft with a young aspiring

Ian McKellan. He shared the stage with, among many others, Peggy Ashcroft, Kenneth Cranham, Frank Finlay, Albert Finney, Michael Gough, Wendy Hiller, Martin Jarvis, Dinsdale Landen, Angela Lansbury, Dandy Nichols, Diana Quick, Denis Quilley, Ralph Richardson, Terence Rigby, Maggie Smith, and Simon Ward. Derek was a close drinking companion and colleague of the great actor Robert Stephens. Peter Hall the distinguished director who succeeded the exalted Laurence Olivier as Director of the National Theatre in 1973, held Derek in high esteem.

Harold Pinter chose Derek to play the lead in probably, the most enigmatic of his plays, and they argued over creative issues. Derek smoked pot with the brilliant American playwright David Mamet, while working with him on the world premier of *Glengarry Glen Ross*, in which Derek delivered his best-ever performance. He was often in a bellicose mood. He once challenged the boisterous and brawny film star Oliver Reed to a fight in a studio canteen. In a Green Room drinking confrontation at the National Theatre, Derek was knocked to the ground by that most perfect of television butlers, Jim Carter, who later won fame as the puritanical Carson in *Downton Abbey*.

Derek was a man of many masks, a master of character: he played the ugliest of Ugly Sisters in the pantomime Cinderella; the most chillingly convincing Martin Bormann, Hitler's henchman, in the Nazi TV drama *Inside the Third Reich*; and he was the very embodiment of Winston Churchill in the controversial stage play *Soldiers*. He was a highly competent comic interpreter: he donned the persona and adopted the mannerisms and witty repartee of both Groucho Marx and W

C Fields to critical acclaim. Derek performed before HM The Queen at the inaugural opening of London's National Theatre in 1976. Some years later at another Royal opening he laughed and drank with Princess Margaret, claiming the unofficial title of 'Keeper of the Royal Ashtray.' Then, having said something out of place, he was roughly ejected from the special event.

Derek was also a regular denizen of Soho, of its pubs, clubs, and cafes. Soho, in those far off days, was a bustling, exciting urban village peopled by Cockney-geezers, street prostitutes, bold and brassy—'Want a good time, Dearie?'—scar-faced foreign ponces, flamboyant painted 'poofs', bibulous writers and actors, and various bohemian characters. It was the age of the afternoon drinking joints, redolent with the macho-aroma of cigarette and cigar smoke, spiced with the exotic waft of weed. Derek's favourite haunts were *The French* pub, the *Coach and Horses*, *Gerry's Club*, the *Caves de France*, the *Kismet Club*, and occasionally he would venture into the scabrous *Colony Room* to exchange insults with its regulars. It was in the latter venue that a young Derek caught the roving, randy eye of the celebrated gay painter Francis Bacon, whose lascivious advances he promptly rejected. Likewise, he told Bacon's promiscuous crony Daniel Farson to 'bugger-off!'

In the 1970s, the newly opened National Theatre building became the dynamo of drama that dominated theatrical London. The purpose-built National complex housed three theatre spaces, the smallest being the home of the legendary Cottesloe Company, a creative, experimental group of players and directors who staged new and often 'impossible' plays and projects. Derek was a founder member and versatile trouper of the Cottesloe crew for ten eventful years, 1975 to 1985. He was a highly valued member, a reliable team player with a rare capacity for comedy. It was during this definitive decade that the mature Derek Newark developed his reputation as a hard-drinking hell-raiser whose bad behaviour was often BANG OUT OF ORDER!

His contentious life story is a tragi-comedy. The Golden Boy of the family, but as the years rolled by, more thinly-gilded than golden... and the gilt rubbed off as he grew older. A born entertainer; actor by nature and profession. A career that began with great expectations, that matured into personal and commercial success... and ended in poverty and premature alcoholic self-destruction. But for divine intervention, fate, kismet, call it what you will, this biography would never have been written. Derek would not have survived infancy. As a toddler he fell into a deep boating-pond at Great Yarmouth. An old lady dressed in black happened to be at the right place at the right time. She fished him out with her umbrella at the very point of death. It was a miracle that he survived without damage to brain or body. We never knew the identity of his guardian angel.

A word of warning to the faint-hearted. There will be—as they say in the world of theatre—some occasional 'bad language' during this performance. I can only say, that to truthfully record Derek's volatile lifespan without recourse to appropriate expletives and raw and vulgar cognomens would be a sanitised travesty. So, put your sensitive soul into neutral and brace yourself for a ride into the talented and turbulent world of Derek Newark...

CHAPTER 2
The Boy with the Golden Voice

Derek was born on 8 June 1933 in Albany Street, Southdown, Great Yarmouth, third and final son of George William and Ella Marie Newark. His siblings were George Kenneth, the eldest, born in London 1928, and myself, Peter Dennis, also born in London in 1931. The newborn was named Derek John, always known to the family as 'Jack'. Our father, George William Newark, born and bred in London, earned an erratic living as an itinerant bookmaker's clerk and tic-tac man, working the race tracks, horse and dogs, throughout southern England. In his younger days, he had danced the boards as a chorus boy in several musical shows, one of which called *Watch Your Step* featured a new kind of syncopated dance music dubbed 'ragtime'.

With the outbreak of the Great War in 1914, George William joined the newly formed Royal Flying Corps (later renamed the Royal Air Force), giving his civilian occupation as 'musical artiste'. On returning to civilian life, he never went back to the stage but chose the unsettled but exciting life of a racing man. He became celebrated as one of the fastest and most reliable tic-tac men in the business. In his prime, he could transmit at racetracks twenty signals in less than five seconds in a rapid blur of hand and arm movements. In later years, he would keep his sons amused and entertained with tales of racecourse villains such as 'Dodger' Mullins and 'Derby' Sabini, and the vicious race-gang battles of the 1920s and 1930s.

In those days, Great Yarmouth had a prosperous herring industry and Dad often called Derek his 'Yarmouth Bloater', a bloater being a herring lightly smoked and salted. In 1939, Dad moved the family back to London, and thence to the suburban town of Romford, Essex, in 1940. In marked contrast to his quieter brothers, Derek displayed an early determination to get up and perform, to be the centre of attention. Aged ten at a local wartime amateur show—billed as 'The Boy with the Golden Voice'—he sang the Vera Lynn song *Silver Wings in the Moonlight* and won a prize. He was indeed the Newark family's golden boy in the making.

At the age of eleven, Derek gained a place at the local Secondary Technical School. He proved a bright pupil and received a decent grounding in English and French. He had by now lost any trace of a Norfolk accent he had picked up in Great Yarmouth. He did not prove to be a brilliant student but he shone on the sports field at football and rugby. He became a leading member of the young committee that chose the films to be shown at the children's Saturday morning matinee at the Plaza cinema, and he was always up front in organizing and presenting any special entertainment.

During the German Blitz on London, which reached out as far as Romford, we boys were thrilled, not frightened, to witness a Messerschmitt 109 fighter roar down Knighton Road at roof-top height and shoot up the big gasometer near the railway track at the bottom of our street. During the regular air raids, Derek and I would have to share a bed together in a bomb shelter.

Some forty years later, when he was a well-known face on television and in the theatre, I would tease him by loudly announcing in a crowded bar or restaurant: 'But, Derek, my dear, you are the only man I've ever slept with!' Curious heads would turn, bitchy ears alert for any showbiz gossip. 'Newark, the tough guy, a nancy?' At first he was annoyed and embarrassed at the jest and endeavoured to explain to those in earshot 'He's my brother...' Later, when he was less protective of his hard-man persona, he came to enjoy the ambiguous joke and we developed the banter.

The teenage Derek grew to be tall and strong. His strapping physique shaped by constant activity on the sports field and by his after school job of peeling buckets of potatoes for a busy local restaurant. But he did not peel the spuds separately with a knife. For several years, Derek and I shared the daily task of peeling potatoes in a cast-iron Victorian machine with a big handle. A large amount of the vegetables was emptied at regular intervals into an open-topped hopper with jagged iron sides, something like a cylindrical cheese-grater—a similar machine called a 'grinder' was used in Victorian prisons as a form of hard labour. You turned the handle and the earth-covered potatoes were thrown against the revolving projections and were eventually skinned in the process. It was tough work, buckets and buckets of peeled spuds. Today such a job would probably be condemned as child abuse, but it was good if boring exercise for growing boys. All for half a crown a week and a hearty dinner in the kitchen of the restaurant after each afternoon session.

Our feckless Dad was not a wealthy man then, and never would be. He was always short of money, and what extra money he did make was soon dissipated on gambling and drinking. At the age of sixteen, Derek decided—or rather family financial difficulties decided for him—to abandon school and higher education for the seemingly adventurous life of the Merchant Navy. He had always yearned to escape the narrow world of suburban Romford and to explore the world. His main goal was New York City, the mecca of the jazz and entertainment culture that we most admired. He joined as a deckhand and although he achieved his ambition of reaching and enjoying his short visit to the city of his dreams—the jazz joints of 52nd Street, Billy Eckstein singing at the Paramount Theatre—he hated the deckhand job and the long voyage getting there, having to literally fight off the persistent advances of a rampant homosexual known as 'Yorkie'. Not exactly the romantic seagoing life that Derek had imagined.

His next job at sea was much better. He was taken on as a trainee steward by the Union Castle Line. His ship the *Capetown Castle* sailed the South Africa round-trip. On his first voyage, he was fortunate enough to be befriended, influenced, and trained by a senior steward named Ronnie Lasch. He was blond, handsome in a Nordic way, charismatic and heterosexual. Ronnie seemed to have had a good education. He sang the Eton Boating Song with old-boy vigour and gave the impression that he had spent time at the school. He taught Derek the finer points of being a superior waiter, in pouring a bottle of wine with the 'Swiss twist' ending, and dressing and serving table silver service. Derek proved a quick and able student, always willing to learn and improve. It was a significant period of social education for him. Ronnie also demonstrated his skill at bullshit in handling and placating all types of awkward passengers. Knowledge that Derek stored in his memory for future use.

Enter old Fred Leaney, like a little leprechaun with his bag of gold coins. Leaney was legend in Romford. An ugly, ginger-haired, bandy-legged bookmaker with his greedy fingers in many nefarious projects. He owned a social club frequented by our Dad; a seedy establishment of shady members who, during the war years had dealt with Leaney in black market goods. The miserly Leaney never spent much money, he hoarded it. In ten years, I never knew him to change his greasy waistcoat and soiled trousers. His personal hygiene was less than fragrant. Leaney's ill-gotten gains included a cache of gold sovereigns—a sovereign being a former British coin having a nominal worth of one pound, and highly valued for its gold content after the introduction of the pound note.

Under the Exchange Control Act of 1947, persons holding sovereigns and other gold coins had to sell them to authorised dealers only. But the avaricious Fred Leaney did not heed the regulation book. He had a paranoic hatred of government bureaucracy so he asked our Dad to put out feelers to see if he could get a better deal in the black economy. Derek came to hear of the plot and passed the information on to his steward friend Ronnie Lasch. He came back with the welcome news that he had good connections in London's Hatton Garden and that he could procure, for a small commission, the highest return available for the sovereigns.

Mean old Leaney trusted Dad, who in turn believed in the sincerity of Ronnie, Derek's clever new friend. The handing over of the large leather pouch of sovereigns took place in our family home in Knighton Road... and that, of course, was the last we ever saw of the persuasive Mr Lasch and the precious bag of gold coins.

Leaney's grasping greed had made him vulnerable. He had been duped. Lasch vanished. Leaney could not, or would not seek retribution on the young conman. For all his wicked ways, Leaney was not a violent man, more miser than mobster. But he would always have a verbal dig at Dad about the affair. Dad on his part never lost the opportunity to berate Derek about that 'thieving ponce... Ronnie fucking Lasch.'

Derek later learned that the slippery Ronnie had settled in New York and had married an American girl. Derek never saw him again, but he never spoke with bitterness about being conned by his old shipmate. He had gained a wealth of worldly knowledge from their relationship. Derek took the philosophical view that it had been an empirical experience, and that Ronnie had been well paid for the lesson. And, after all, it wasn't Derek's money.

On leaving the Merchant Navy and in pursuit of his ambition to become a professional solo comedian, Derek took several transient jobs in order to pay his everyday way. He became assistant salesman in the high street shop of Lew Diamond, Bespoke Tailor. Lew was a Jewish gentleman of liberal outlook. A rotund, well-dressed, man-of-the-world, and a very cheeky chappie on occasion. Derek and Diamond bonded almost immediately. To ease the tedium of the day, Lew told Derek Jewish jokes and stories, and would pull certain comic stunts. On a rainy day, while measuring a customer for a suit, he would mumble with a straight face, 'Shall I tickle your arse with a feather, sir?' When the bemused punter asked, 'What did you say?' Diamond would carefully enunciate, 'It's particularly nasty weather, sir.' Derek would turn away, smothering his laughter.

Working with Diamond proved to be a master-class in Jewish culture. Lew didn't make his bespoke suits and coats on the premises. He despatched Derek into London's East End workshops with his sartorial orders, and to bring back completed items. Derek enjoyed these business trips. He soaked up Yiddish words and phrases, studying Jewish gestures and mannerisms. He used the shop floor as he would later use a rehearsal hall. Again, he learned a lot about a certain aspect of working life that would come in useful in his future acting career. In later years, Derek would do a hilarious but affectionate imitation of that fine actor David Kossoff, in a satirical send-up of the Kossoff film *The Bespoke Overcoat* (1955).

As teenagers, Derek and I became fans of a new jazz movement called 'bebop' or 'bop' that blew in from America during the late 1940s, its revolutionary messengers being the musicians Charlie Parker and Dizzy Gillespie. In London, the early bebop banner was taken up by a group headed by Ronnie Scott and Johnny Dankworth. The leading bop venues were the *Feldman Club* in Oxford Street and the *Club Eleven* in Gerrard Street. It was at the Feldman place that we befriended a semi-professional jazz drummer who had a day job selling insurance and harboured a burning ambition to be a playwright. His name was Johnny Speight.

BANG OUT OF ORDER!

Derek and Johnny quickly developed a close affinity. Both were eager to make their mark in show business, Derek as a comedian, Johnny as a wordsmith. They got together in mutual endeavour. Johnny came to the family home in Knighton Road a number of times to work with Derek on a solo routine. I sat and listened, fascinated by Johnny's fertile imagination and Derek's volatile reaction. One particular gag that Speight created at this time has stuck in my mind ever since. Its subject was Victor Sylvester, the celebrated ballroom dancer-teacher and strict-tempo bandleader of radio fame. Johnny's joke was a word play on Sylvester's quick-step patter: 'Quick, quick, quick-quick slow.' Johnny had Victor looking out of a window on a white Christmas, saying: 'Thick, thick, thick-thick snow!'

Nothing permanent came of the early Newark-Speight collaboration. They went their separate ways. The main reason being that Speight, the puppet-master, wanted to mould Derek into a Cockney barrow-boy character, whereas Derek had a vastly different vision of his desired stage persona. He saw himself as a sophisticated purveyor of funny stories and a few songs, a less frantic version of Danny Kaye. Johnny progressed to writing gags and scripts for top comedians such as Frankie Howard and Peter Sellars. He did, however, re-cycle the Sylvester gag at a later date in his career—nothing is forgotten or wasted in the writing game—in the radio show *Mr Ros and Mr Ray*, starring bandleaders Edmundo Ros and Ray Ellington, of whom Johnny said: 'They couldn't act and they could hardly talk proper [sic]... so any big words would have been lost, not only on the audience but on them [sic] as well. I did about five gags per show and got £15 a week.'

BANG OUT OF ORDER!

Johnny Speight was a rare bird in the literary sense. Most professional writers that I have known, well educated or working-class, were fluent speakers with an extensive vocabulary; their thoughtful prose a continuation of their clear verbal output. Johnny, by marked contrast, suffered a speech impediment, a soft stutter compounded by a strangulated Cockney accent, punctuated by far too many 'Know what I mean?' He was difficult enough to understand when calm and collected, but when he became excited or agitated by some sudden creative idea, or if he became locked into a heated political debate, he spoke so rapidly and with such ardour that the garbled machine-gun words shot out in a continuous stream impossible to interpret.

But sitting at his typewriter, Johnny became another person. His creative talent took control. He became the popular communicator, choosing his words carefully to skilfully express his comic ideas and funny dialogue. Johnny gained national fame and fortune by creating the loud-mouthed, working-class bigot Alf Garnett in the long-running BBC Television sitcom *Till Death Us Do Part* (1964-74) and its sequel *In Sickness and in Health* (1985-86). He also created many plays and other comedy series. However, talented writer that he was, the canny producers of his shows always relied heavily on educated and experienced script editors to knock his rough material into proper shape for broadcasting. He once modestly said, albeit with a Marxist bias, of his greatest creation Alf Garnett: 'I didn't really create Alf... our rotten society did. I just grassed him up.' The term 'grassed' being Cockney for 'informed on him'.

Johnny had achieved all that he had aspired to all those years ago sitting in our parlour at Knighton Road. By the 1990s,

BANG OUT OF ORDER!

his long run of success came to an end. His comic concoctions were not politically correct. He fell out of fashion and was dropped by the sensitive BBC and he more or less retired from the game. He had amassed a fortune and enjoyed his latter years as an elder statesman of comedy writers. He died in 1998 aged 78. Although Derek's acting career took him in a different show business direction, he did run into Johnny many times over the years for a drink and a chat, usually at the BBC when they were both working there. He did not come into Speight's professional orbit until 1989, when Derek was cast as a blue-blazer-wearing bore in Johnny's last TV series, about a private golf club, called *The Nineteenth Hole*.

Back in the early 1950s, Derek, the apprentice comedian, embraced poorly paid and unpaid gigs whenever he could in the local area, and sometimes in parts of London: stag-parties, talent shows, even village hall fetes. Each event was an opportunity to polish and perfect his burgeoning capacity to entertain and make people laugh. Every stage appearance increased his inner confidence as a solo performer. He was now, in his own estimation, no longer a raw amateur but a semi-professional.

In August 1953, Derek entered a talent competition, *Stars of Tomorrow*, held at a local cinema. He was the only comedian on the bill. The others were a mixed bag of singers, dancers, a magician, and a truly awful mime act. Derek's material comprised vocal and visual gags he had appropriated from star comics he admired, especially Jack Benny and Bob Hope. All second-hand stuff, but with one prize-winning exception. England had just beaten Australia for the Ashes, the first

BANG OUT OF ORDER!

time since 1933. Derek came on stage smoking a cigarette in extravagant style, tapping the ash repeatedly into his carefully cupped left hand. After a brief silence, he surveyed the house and loudly announced—'Must keep the Ashes, you know!' Loud applause from the patriotic audience. It was an original gag that he had conjured up at the last moment on hearing the news on the radio. It won him the competition.

CHAPTER 3
An Officer and a Comedian

Derek's young life was changed significantly when he received his National Service call-up papers in September 1953, with instructions to report for duty at the Brigade of Guards Depot at Caterham, Surrey. He was twenty years old, six feet tall, and of robust physique. He joined the ranks of the training battalion of the Coldstream Guards—motto *Nulli Secundas*: 'Second to None'. He gave his civilian occupation as 'Variety Artiste', just like his father had done in 1915.

On first parade, the drill sergeant soon picked him out.

'And what kind of variety "arteest" were you?' he snapped.

'A comedian, Sergeant,' Derek replied.

'A comedian, you say. Then make me laugh,' he said.

'I'm not that clever, Sarge, I'm only a comic—not a miracle worker!' Derek replied with a wry smile, thinking that the grim-faced NCO would appreciate his sense of humour. Wrong. The NCO just glared back hard faced.

Derek had made his first military mistake. Other ranks, especially raw recruits, should never attempt to out-smart, or appear to be too clever when replying verbally to a person of superior rank, commissioned officer or not. If they do they will regret it. And so it came to pass with Derek. The drill sergeant decided, in agreement with some other NCOs, to knock the cockiness out of the gabby comedian and henceforth they made his life a misery. Extra drill. Extra fatigues. Extra this, extra that, all on top of the regular tough training routine. This continued to such an extent that Derek, harassed and hounded, decided to desert and run away from the exhausting ordeal.

He managed to get out of the camp undetected, but a few hours later he had serious second thoughts about his desperate situation. He decided to return to the 'bear-pit' and endure the baiting. He would 'beat the bastards' at their own game—endure and overcome, like a proper Guardsman. He resolved to become the perfect soldier. He would march better than the other recruits. He would salute more sharply. He walked with a notable martial gait when not on parade. His kit was smarter than the others. His voice, when called upon, was loud and clear, delivered in the required military tone. He made himself stand out in the new intake. His tormentors relented and he was promoted to Lance Corporal (two stripes in the Guards) and given the task of drilling raw recruits. Derek was on the first rung of the army ladder.

In June 1954, Lance Corporal Newark played a small walk-on part in that popular theatrical event of military excellence, Trooping the Colour, at London's Horse Guards Parade in the presence of HM Queen Elizabeth. This most spectacular display, involving the Foot Guards and the Household Cavalry in full dress uniforms, marks the annual celebration of the Sovereign's Official Birthday, in which the five regiments of Guards take it in turn to troop, or parade, their special 'Colour' or regimental flag. Derek was always proud of his small role in this traditional ceremony. Indeed, he was always proud of being a Coldstreamer.

Recommended as a potential officer, Derek was sent to a War Office Selection Board (WOSB) for initial assessment. He seemed to be on the way up. Excited and stimulated at the prospect of a commission, he prepared himself for the demanding role. He had already modified his London/Essex accent. Now, he began to choose and carefully enunciate his words; he clipped and pruned his hitherto rapid manner of speech. The days of Cockney-geezer comic were over (but not to be entirely forgotten). A golden opportunity had presented itself and he dearly wanted the part. Now for the momentous audition.

The WOSB ('Wosbee') panel of officers put him through a preliminary series of intelligence and general knowledge tests. He seemed to be doing very well in this Grand National of a tricky course, clearing question after question, until he came to a 'Becher's Brook' of a challenge. 'As an officer you will be required to give lectures, and to express yourself correctly in conversation with your peers and superiors. How would you articulate these particular words, and can you further explain their meaning?'

A sheet of paper was placed before him bearing the noun 'epitome' and the adjective 'omnipotent'. He mispronounced both words, but to his credit gave a clear understanding of their meaning. He never forgot his humiliation and, as he said to me, 'I never forgot those two bloody words!'

Having failed the shibboleth test, his misery was compounded when his schooling was deemed unsatisfactory, not meeting the required criterion. One snooty officer declared 'On paper you are clearly uneducated'. Derek was on the brink of rejection, but again it seemed divine providence came to his rescue. A veteran colonel of the board, who had risen from the rank and file, had taken a shine to the bright young Guardsman. He had witnessed enough 'posh' failures in the past, despite their coming from the right schools and correct backgrounds. The colonel knew that becoming an officer was a complex course of events in the military school of learning. He saw beyond Derek's two-word deficiency. He approved of his composure under pressure and had noted his already mature and martial manner. He could sense an officer in the making, a potential leader of men. Turning to Major 'Snooty', he said firmly 'We'll give him all the further education that he needs. I believe this man to be a promising candidate.' The colonel influenced the others and Derek passed the 'Wosbee' grilling. The audition was over. He had got the part. Now for the rigours of rehearsal.

On 8 October 1954, Derek was posted to Mons Officer Cadet School at Aldershot. He bade farewell to his ramrod Coldstreamers, but his Foot Guards ethos of bullshit drill and brilliance never left his psyche and proved an invaluable asset to his future theatrical career. Again, at Mons, he determined to be the best of his intake and he carried the top-cadet sword at the Passing Out Parade on 19 November 1954. Derek had been fortunate, in a minor historical sense, to have experienced the last days at Mons of the living legend that was Regimental Sergeant Major Ronald Brittain, celebrated as possessing the 'Loudest Voice in the Army'.

BANG OUT OF ORDER!

RSM Brittain of the Coldstream Guards had spent a decade drilling officer cadets at Mons. He was a martinet of the old school; a formidable advocate of 'Nothing is good enough but the very best'. A giant of a man, six feet four and 18 stone of Foot Guards spit and polish, he was both ogre and mentor to the thousands of officer cadets that he drilled and bollocked with his stentorian voice. He would give the same short introductory lecture on discipline and Mons protocol to all new intakes that included the warning: 'While you are here I shall address each of you as "sir". You shall address me at all times as "Sir"—the difference being that YOU WILL MEAN IT!'

To be singled-out and personally upbraided by Brittain came to be viewed by the unfortunate cadets involved as a rite of passage, an anecdote to be repeated and exaggerated at future Mess dinners. Derek came face to face with Brittain on several parade occasions and passed his gimlet-eyed inspection without comment. Derek heard many actual and apocryphal stories about Brittain. He told me about the rare incident when the remarkable RSM made a comical faux pas. At the time the ageing eyes of the RSM were not as sharp as they used to be. He wore spectacles for reading, but never on parade. Early one frosty morning when drilling cadets in his usual roaring manner, he spotted something out of order in the middle of the front rank.

'That cadet! Take your gloves off, sir!'

Not a body moved.

'That cadet wearing gloves! Take them off!'

Still no movement in the front rank. An irate Brittain, pace-stick under his arm, marched grimly towards the man in question. When he crunched to a Coldstream halt, he realised the enormity of his error. The cadet was not wearing brown gloves—he happened to be an Indian.

After Mons, Derek was posted to Cadet Company 1, The Royal Army Service Corps (RASC) at Aldershot. Again, he came top of his Cadet Course, which included an arduous survival test of endurance in the wilderness of Wales. He later told me that his training in the Guards and the RASC survival course were the most physically demanding period of his five years in the army. Derek was appointed Parade Second-in-Command Junior Under Officer for the Passing Out Parade and Commissioning Service of 18 March 1955. Second Lieutenant Derek John Newark was now a professional soldier, a regular, with a three-year short-service commission and an option of a further five years to follow.

The Royal Army Service Corps was formally established in 1794 as the Corps of Waggoners, raised to carry military supplies to regimental camps and battle zones. Over 200 years, through many campaigns and two world wars, it grew into a great corps that transported and supplied all army units throughout the world with food, ammunition, fuel, road and air transportation, animals when required, and multifarious military stores. In 1965, the RASC became the Royal Corps of Transport. In 1993, the title changed again to the Royal Logistic Corps. In Derek's time the regimental march was *Wait for the Wagon* and I believe it remains so to this day.

*****

Derek was posted to Singapore and his arrival there was recorded in *The Waggoner*, the regimental journal, of June 1955. The Federation of Malaya, formed of British colonial possessions, was then a cockpit of armed conflict, containing large British military bases. Kuala Lumpur, known to the troops as 'KL', was its chief city.

When the Federation of Malaya was formed in February 1948, its infant authority was challenged and undermined by armed elements of the revived Communist Party that had been outlawed by the British in the early 1930s. This rebel force called itself the 'Malayan Races Liberation Army' (MRLA). Malaya and Singapore had mixed race populations, with the Malays and the Chinese being predominant. In this volatile struggle for power, the rebel forces were widely aided and abetted by the Chinese faction, especially in the jungle regions. The British Army supported the legal Malayan Government, its police force and soldiers, referring at first to these armed insurgents as 'bandits' and later as 'communist terrorists' (CTs) because they carried out acts of sabotage, intimidation and murder of native workers in tin mines and rubber estates. These victims later included Europeans and British army personnel.

The campaign against the communist forces was officially called a 'State of Emergency' and the RASC played a vital role in supplying the sinews of war to the many British units involved from 1948 to 1960, when hostilities ended. Many British regiments served in the fight to save Malaya and Singapore from the Red menace. Among them the Royal Artillery, the Brigade of Guards, several infantry regiments, six Ghurka battalions, and units of the SAS. The RASC was, at first, understaffed and thinly spread, covering an area from Selangor south of KL to as far north as Tapah Perak, and the Cameron Highlands. The RASC School at Nee Soon Singapore was organised to train native recruits drawn from all races in Malaya. Among many other duties, the RASC supplied the troop-carrying requirements of infantry units engaged in jungle operations, and the provision of suitable ration packs for the Ghurkas and Malay soldiers to carry on these combat missions. As the tempo of operations increased and spread with more troops moving into the jungle away from their regimental bases, supply by aircraft became the main operational function of the RASC throughout the campaign.

To aid the infantry in following the trails left by the CTs the British recruited Iban trackers from North Borneo, natural experts in tracing both animals and humans in the jungle.

'How do you communicate with the Iban?' enquired a nosy Malayan civil service officer of a young British lieutenant on his return from jungle patrol. 'Have you learned their language?'

The lieutenant shrugged.

'No. We use English.'

The civil service officer was now very curious.

'How much have they learned?'

'Enough for us. I'll give you a demonstration.'

He called a tracker by name and the man came forward. The lieutenant pointed to the ground and jumped about on the spot, leaving a mess of jumbled footprints. The tracker, whose English had been picked up from rank and file squaddies, knelt down and spoke grim-faced.

'Not fooking good.'

The lieutenant then moved to another spot and left a single heel-print in the dirt. The Iban examined the mark, pointed in the right direction, and proclaimed with a broad smile.

'Fooking good!'

The lieutenant turned to the baffled civil servant.

'That's quite good enough for us.'

Derek served in Malaya from June 1955 to May 1958. His duties included the maintenance and protection of supply lines comprised of trucks, jeeps, ambulances, and mules, through jungle tracks and vulnerable open roads. Enemy ambushes were a constant hazard. Sir Henry Gurney, High Commissioner of Malaya, was killed in one. Derek proved more than competent at his task and in June 1956 was promoted First Lieutenant, with two 'pips' or stars on his shoulder strap. When the RASC formed a jungle patrol, under the command of the Coldstream Guards, to search out and destroy CT camps, Derek, a former Coldstreamer, volunteered for this dangerous patrol.

After he left the army he rarely spoke to me about this jungle experience. Once, however, when I pressed him on the matter he did confess that patrolling the hostile rain forest was:

> The most frightening time of my life. Especially at night, creeping along a narrow track, pistol in hand, uniform soaked in sweat, eyes and ears constantly alert, not knowing what to expect at any moment, hacking through dense undergrowth... Danger lurking everywhere. Not only from fanatical CTs but from deadly snakes and fucking-great hornets whose sting could paralyse a man.

His lips were sealed on the subject of special operations by his signing the Official Secrets Act.

Some years after he had left the army, when he was being interviewed by a show business journalist, Derek uncharacteristically let slip the following brief information: 'Yes, I served in Malaya, some of it on special duties I can't talk about until 25 years are up... All I can say is I was involved in some pretty "hairy" situations.' When I had lunch a few years back with a fellow-officer and friend who had served with Derek in Malaya, and I probed about these special duties, he just mumbled something about the Official Secrets Act and changed the subject to Derek's funny side and his prowess on the rugby field. I did not press the subject.

One graphic incident of Derek's mysterious jungle war did emerge from under the cloak of silence some twenty years after the event. Jack Shepherd and Keith Dewhurst co-authored a book, *Impossible Plays*, all about the Cottesloe Company of the National Theatre, of which Derek was a founder member. Shepherd recalls in the book a frightening incident when he shared a dressing room with Derek in 1978. Jack was appearing in the play *American Buffalo* in the Cottesloe theatre and Derek in *Bedroom Farce* at the Lyttelton, which ended some twenty minutes after *American Buffalo*. Shepherd, too exhausted to clean the fake blood from his face, fell half-asleep in his chair, his visage a red mask of death. Next thing he knew he was shaken awake by a shout of anguish and being knocked to the floor and smothered by a dark coat—with Derek on top apparently trying to suffocate him!

Shepherd struggled hard to free himself and finally Derek

released his deadly grip. Derek was now in a state of shocked remorse and bewilderment. He apologised profusely and endeavoured to explain his crazy assault, the cause of which reached back over twenty years to his war service in Malaya. During a jungle night patrol to search out and pacify communist insurgents, Derek came into close combat with the enemy and inflicted a mortal stomach wound on a man, who did not die immediately. Derek, stricken with acute compassion, spent the rest of the night nursing and consoling his victim, who died at dawn. When Derek entered the dressing room and saw Shepherd's bloody face, it brought back in a flash the horrid death scene in the jungle. In his moment of madness, he was, he explained, trying to save the 'dying' actor—not kill him! Anyway, that was the reason given to the severely shaken Shepherd. An apparent case of post-traumatic stress disorder some twenty years after a shocking event.

*****

Army life was not all duty and danger for Derek. He played lots of football and rugby. He was captain of his rugby team and later became Secretary of the Regimental RFC of Singapore. He learned to fence and to ride a horse, both skills he would further develop for use in his acting career. At every opportunity he organised, presented, and took part in numerous regimental concerts to entertain the troops.

'As well as all this,' he wrote home, 'I manage to wangle time for my solo routine in nightclubs, and I have my own comedy show on Singapore radio. I use the pseudonym "Jackie Styles" as I don't want the top brass finding out about my "secret" activities. My close chums know and they keep "mum".'

In fact, Derek lived two lives in Singapore: Lieutenant DJ Newark on Her Majesty's Service during the day, and London comedian Jackie Styles in off-duty hours. In his military capacity he headed the Committee that organised and presented the Christmas Ball entertainment of 1956 in aid of the British Red Cross Society of Singapore, held at the famous Raffles Hotel—and he also compered the show. In April 1957, he hosted the *Francis Vernon's On Stage* entertainment at the Victoria Memorial Hall and received the following critical review: 'Jackie Styles was a very good compere. But here is a word of advice to him—he should check himself (or somebody should check him) not to make offensive remarks about the audience.'

Radio Malaya English reported on its upcoming 1957 *Easter Fair* show:

> Two new stars in the entertainment world will come before the Malayan microphone for the first time. One of them will be the attractive Spanish film, radio and TV star Teresita de Alba... The other newcomer is wise-cracking Jackie Styles, and if anybody can teach you how to laugh, he certainly can.

The *Spotlight* column in *The Straits Times* of 28 April 1957 heralded:

> Another pleasing newcomer was comedian Jackie Styles who kept the studio audience laughing throughout his act. Malayan [radio] listeners only too rarely hear comedians, and a good one is therefore the more welcome when he makes an appearance.

BANG OUT OF ORDER!

By this stage of his covert comic career, Derek had found a catchphrase: 'Laughs and Smiles with Jackie Styles.' Here's a couple of sample gags from the Styles comic routine.

'I must say I do like a drink,' said Derek. 'And whenever I raise my glass, I toast my uncle, who taught me that you should always stop drinking when you can't spell your own name backwards. A clever man... cheers to you Uncle BOB!'

'Yes, Uncle Bob was a naughty boy,' carried on Derek. 'Always in trouble with the law. His latest escapade earned him an ultimatum from the judge: join the army or go to jail. He chose the army.'

Derek would then pause for either cheers or jeers from a service audience.

'Six months after enlisting, his mother receives a letter from Bob. She turns to her husband: "George, how long did it take Montgomery to reach Field Marshal?" George scratched his head and said "Some thirty years, I think." Mother smiled and handed him the letter, saying "I'm so proud of Bob. Only six months in the army and already he's up for COURT MARTIAL!"'

The Rediffusion *Times of Singapore* reported in its *Programme News* for Christmas 1957 a special performance by the Combined Services Entertainment Unit headed by comedian Stan Stennett:

> Stan was recently top of the bill at the London Palladium, the very heart of show business. His broadcast for Rediffusion constitutes his ONLY public appearance in Malaya and Singapore, his tour having been confined to Army camps.

BANG OUT OF ORDER!

Then directly below the Stan Stennett item, Rediffusion proclaimed:

> JACK'S BACK! Jackie Styles, who supplied the laughs in the recent Eno 'Variety Fanfare' programme, makes a speciality of poking gentle fun at human foibles. A frequent broadcaster over Rediffusion, he can also be heard as 'Gabby Halliday' in the weekly cowboy programme 'On The Trail'.

It's interesting to note that Derek became close friends with fellow-officer Derek Agutter who was also stationed in Singapore, and he ran the Combined Services Entertainment Unit of which he later became the leading figure. He organised a special show for the British troops stationed in the Falkland Islands during the war of 1982. Derek kept in touch with Agutter over the intervening years and helped him out in a tight spot by supervising several tours of overseas army camps. Derek Agutter is the father of Jenny Agutter, star of stage, film and television, who as a child lived with her father in Malaya.

When not entertaining the public as his civilian alter ego Jackie Styles, Lieutenant Derek Newark greatly enjoyed the traditional rituals of the Officers' Mess. For special dinners, he relished donning mess kit and sitting at the table gleaming with candles and regimental silver. After dinner, the younger men would indulge in rough and tumble games such as High Cockalorum and British Bulldog, at which rugby-playing Derek excelled. He told me a story that captures the jolly banter of the Mess. A colonel greeted a new young subaltern to the regiment.

'You'll like it here, Carew, our Mess nights are always fun. On Monday we play poker and...'

'I don't gamble, sir,' Carew interrupted.

'Ah, well,' said the colonel. 'On Tuesday we have the best Cuban cigars.'

'I don't smoke, sir, never have.'

'I see,' mused the colonel. 'Perhaps Wednesday will suit you. Malt whiskey...'

'I don't drink, sir.'

'On Thursday,' continued the colonel, 'we have certain ladies from the town to entertain us... If you get my drift.'

'I don't go with loose women, sir,' answered Carew with distaste.

At this the colonel exploded.

'You're not queer, are yer laddie?'

'Certainly not, sir!'

'Then you won't like Friday night either!' said the colonel.

Derek did not come home on leave during his three years in the Far East, preferring instead to explore more of Southeast Asia in his off-duty time. He met his future wife, Jean Thornhill, in September 1955 at a dance organised by the Royal Education Corps for officers and teachers at a school hall in Singapore. Derek was immediately impressed by the tall and gentle teacher from Yorkshire. But Jean, however, was not instantly enamoured by his brash and forthright manner. Nevertheless, he persisted in his courtship and won her over and she came to love him dearly. They spent many joyous days together in Singapore, Kuala Lumpur, and Hong Kong. Jean, a cultured lady, considered KL to be:

The most beautiful city... the railway station built like an oriental palace... handsome white public buildings, a strange amalgam of English Gothic and Moorish architectural styles... the native quarter an exotic and romantic place... The bustling and bounteous markets, the babel of many tongues and diverse dialects of Indians, Malays, and Chinese. The strange, extravagant smells of spices, fruits, and meat cooking in the streets. So different to pale and shabby England.

In Hong Kong, Derek and Jean visited all the tourist sights of the island city, in those days still a British colony, and savoured the finest Chinese cuisine. They picnicked and sunbathed on the beach and swam in the calm waters of Repulse Bay, and they shouted encouragement to their chosen horses on the racetrack at Happy Valley. Their Far East idyll together was the happiest times of their lives.

The Independent Federation of Malaya was formed in 1957. In June of that year, Derek was promoted to Acting Captain. In March 1958, he was discharged to the Regular Army Reserve of Officers. Two months later, he left Singapore for England, his departure recorded in *The Waggoner* of May 1958. Jean followed him home and they married. Derek had decided against signing on for another five years. He had seen enough of military life. Had he pursued his army career, he could very well have attained high rank, but he said to me 'I came out because I didn't want to spend the rest of my life as a professional killer.'

In 1963, the Federation of Malaysia came into being, a

democratic state formed by the amalgamation of Malaya, Sarawak and Sabah, with Kuala Lumpur its capital. The city-state of Singapore became an independent republic in 1965 and today has the highest standard of living in Southeast Asia. An enviable situation made possible by the 12-year campaign waged mainly by British forces in repelling a communist takeover. Derek came home without a campaign medal, but with the knowledge that he had done his duty in the making of a free and democratic nation—a war not recognised as such, but as a 'State of Emergency'. He was entitled to the General Service Medal with 'Malaya' clasp.

He did, however, make a ghostly curtain call when he received a posthumous award for services rendered. In February 2011, his son, Quentin, accepted a long-awaited medal on his father's behalf from the hands of the grateful Ambassador of Malaysia. This medal called the Pingat Jasa Malaysia translates as 'Award for Aiding Malaysia'. The ambassador addressed a gathering of some sixty veterans, including Ghurkas, thanking them and the spirits of comrades who had passed on for 'coming to the aid of my fledgling country... and Malaysia today, although not perfect, is a peaceful democracy, with a multi-racial population, in a volatile region where ethnic tolerance and the right to vote are not common.' Cue audience applause. Derek Newark, and a cast of thousands, step forward and take a bow.

CHAPTER 4
Training at RADA

Back in civvy street, Derek decided on a new career in show business. Not as a solo comedian, but as an actor. It was time for Shakespeare, Sheridan and Shaw and all the other deities of drama and satire. But could he do it? Would he be good enough to make the grade in a highly competitive profession? He was twenty-five years old, somewhat late to begin a new trade. And rather than plunging-in untutored at the deep end, he determined on a classical training at London's Royal Academy of Dramatic Art (RADA).

Derek married Jean Thornhill in April 1958 and they started married life together living at his parents' home in Knighton Road, a small terraced house in Romford, now in the northeast London Borough of Havering. Returning to civvy street after five years of overseas military life was a significant culture change. With the singular exception of his jungle experience, Derek had lived the comfortable life of an officer and a gentleman, an ordered life of perks and privilege. From a secure and regulated existence in a closely stratified community, he had returned to an open society of hard commercial and competitive enterprise. No more batman servant, no more grand mess dinners, no more army accommodation, and no more free transport and travel. Derek Newark, married man, must now face the world armed only with his promising talent, a rough talent that he must polish and present for public judgement.

He came out of the army with a £400 gratuity. Jean found a post at a local school, teaching young children. To make ends meet, Derek took on various mundane jobs and did some comedy gigs as Jackie Styles, but he had grown weary of the routine gag performance. He could foresee a better, wider, more demanding future on the legitimate stage. An actor he would be. He approached the Royal Academy of Dramatic Art and impressed them enough that, although they could not provide a free scholarship, they could offer him a place as a private student. He circumvented this potential financial burden by winning an Essex Education Committee award that covered the full cost of all his fees and began his classical training at RADA in January 1959 on a two-year course.

RADA was founded in 1904 by Sir Herbert Beerbohm Tree and was granted its Royal Charter in 1920 by HM King George V, thus conferring for the first time a very special honour such as no institution for training in the art of drama in Britain has ever enjoyed. Hundreds of famous actors of stage and screen have trained there. In Derek's time, the distinguished Principal was John Fernald, appointed to the post in 1955. He was first an actor and subsequently a producer of many plays. The Academy's curriculum embraced Singing, Voice Production, Shakespeare Speaking, Audition Technique, Acting, Mime, Broadcasting, Film, Movement, Stage Deportment, and Fencing. RADA's own theatre, the Vanbrugh, was situated nearby in Malet Street.

BANG OUT OF ORDER!

Derek's first student report contained the following comments from his respective tutors and the Principal:

VOICE PRODUCTION: Unfortunately you have not yet completely conquered your 'r' difficulties, but they are only glaringly apparent when associated with explosives! You tend to pinch your tone and this only renders it thinner than it is. Work for more rhythmic speech.

SHAKESPEARE SPEAKING: A splendid student, excellent stage manager, and a very good attempt at Mercutio. I should have been lost without him. Work on voice, breathing and carry through to the ends of lines.

ACTING: The Diary of a Scoundrel. Derek is a joy to work with. He has a very real and true instinct for comedy... He thinks of the character and the play before obvious comic effect, and takes criticism and uses it to his advantage. I have only seen him do comedy, but I am sure he is not a limited actor. There is no doubt to my mind that he belongs in the theatre and has a lot to give to it.

JOHN FERNALD: Your good work continues. Watch out for the occasional faulty vowel sound. It trips you up and is noticeable particularly because your diction for the most part is so good.

Derek's second report showed continuous good progress:

VOICE PRODUCTION: You are coming along well. Your speech defect has really been conquered although there must always be an awareness on your part of those occasions when it is liable to recur. You must study the text for linguistic difficulties.

AUDITION TECHNIQUE: This student has worked splendidly and has done a variety of audition pieces, all of them a success. He has already acquired a good deal of technical assurance, and presents himself well.

A MIDSUMMER NIGHT'S DREAM: This student's performance as Bottom was quite excellent and showed his valuable comedy gifts. He made the character as well as the clown come to life. His Theseus, though good, lacked the confidence for the required 'light' comedy and showed a shortcoming in his speech work, which, with his ability to work, will soon be rectified.

THE CONSTANT NYMPH: I like this student's work very much indeed. He has a proper professional approach towards it, works extremely hard and played a range of character parts with skill and feeling...

TECHNIQUE: A full-blooded and vigorous comedian who still makes one or two basic mistakes. He must not allow his voice to fade out so regularly at the ends of sentences. He must watch out for remaining gaucheries in movement (leaving one leg behind, for example).

JOHN FERNALD: Excellent work as always. I look forward to your work in Finals.

In his third report Derek is still having difficulties with his diction:

VOICE PRODUCTION: Naughty over the 'r'. It really should have been mastered by now... Is it a 'gimmick'?

ACTING: I cannot urge you strongly enough to work more harder on your diction and other vocal problems. Your habit, for example, of dropping your voice to the point of inaudibility at the end of sentences ruined what might otherwise have been good performances as George Kettle [in Mr Kettle and Mrs Moon by JB Priestly] and Clive Popkiss [in Rookery Nook by Ben Travers]. You have very definite talent as a comedian and have developed great technical efficiency at 'getting laughs'. This cannot be praised too highly, but I do urge you to study your parts with infinitely greater care than is your present habit...

JOHN FERNALD: Difficulties of diction remain in plenty, and you will not reach first-class achievement until you have completely solved them. None the less you came nearer to solving them in Rookery Nook than ever before, and I hope next term will see you well on the way to being really good.

The next and final term was due to begin on 3 October 1960, but before then the RADA Players, including Derek, enjoyed a successful summer season at the Little Theatre at Bangor, Northern Ireland. They opened on 4 July 1960 and performed a varied programme of seven plays, each with a six-week run. The first being *Rookery Nook,* then *Mr Kettle and Mrs Moon*, followed by *I Captured the Castle* by Dodie Smith. Next came *The Hollow* by Agatha Christie, followed by *For Better For*

Worse by Arthur Watkyn, *Sabrina Fair* by Samuel Taylor, and finally *Pygmalion* by George Bernard Shaw.

In Dodie Smith's adaptation of *I Captured the Castle* from her best-selling novel of the same name, a local reviewer noted that 'In minor roles, too, we had some delightful characterisations, including Derek Newark's clever study of the vicar, which stood out for its touch of realness.' Another local critic said of *For Better For Worse* 'Derek Newark and Hilary Newcombe once again demonstrated their versatility as the bride's parents. Despite the lack of opportunities to star—theirs were the best realised performances.' Another reviewer added 'Derek Newark is a very adaptable actor and gave a distinguished performance as the father.' Derek's finest performance of the season came in Shaw's *Pygmalion*. *The Belfast Telegraph* commented: 'Derek Newark is one of the best cast members and he scores a great hit with his portrayal of Alfred Doolittle, the dustman.' Bangor theatre critic Betty Lowry wrote: 'The part of Doolittle, the dustman, who confesses to being "one of the deserving poor" is a gift for any actor. Derek Newark makes the most of it. He looks, sounds, and is an incredibly rascally, scheming, original and likeable character.'

Back at RADA, Derek received his final report for the Autumn Term 1960:

> VOICE PRODUCTION: I think you have made great progress during your time with me. Your voice has more weight and if the speech is sometimes troublesome, I know you are aware of the need to get this right.
> ACTING: Dear Brutus. I like Derek's acting—he has a

good sense of character and a firm line through whatever he does. I was very pleased with his performance as Matey.
JOHN FERNALD: You have made very good use of your two years and I think you will do very well indeed. Please go on working for clarity—and watch those 'R's—and you'll get better and better. You have been awarded a Diploma.

Derek had made a close chum of fellow student Roger Jerome and they partnered each other in the Fencing Competition, winning the coveted award. After RADA they kept in touch and both appeared in *The Three Musketeers* at the Nottingham Playhouse in 1962, in which Derek played Porthos and Roger had the role of Rochefort, the villain. Both of them instructed the other actors in the skill of fencing and they stage-managed the spectacular sword-fighting scenes. Roger later went to America and forged a career as a drama teacher. He never forgot Derek, who had kept him laughing throughout their student years together. Other alumni at RADA for the year 1959-60 included Ken Campbell, Alan Lake, June Richie, Sarah Badel, Sheila Gish, John Hurt, Martin Jarvis, Gemma Jones, Lynda La Plante, George Layton, John Alderton, Terence Rigby, Ian McShane and David Warner.

Derek greatly valued his training at RADA, especially the time and effort spent in correcting his flawed diction. He learned to speak clearly and to project his voice to the backseats of the audience. Nowadays it seems that young aspiring actors are not trained, or do not think it necessary, to master this basic discipline, and because there's so much work in television it appears that clarity of speech doesn't matter anymore. The mumble brigade has taken over TV drama. If Derek were alive today I'm sure he would have joined the many protests of veteran, and properly trained, actors such as Sir Derek Jacobi and Dame Penelope Keith who have openly criticised this modern mode of mumbling.

In an interview published in *The Stage* and picked-up by *The Daily Telegraph* in November 2014, Jacobi said he struggled to understand many young actors and that speaking clearly should be the 'bedrock' of their craft. He claimed that modern drama schools produced students who sought quick fame and celebrity rather than 'learning their job.' Edward Kemp, the director of RADA, responded that the efforts of actors to enunciate properly were often thwarted by directors who preferred 'naturalistic' dialogue to 'old-fashioned' speaking.

Penelope Keith joined the protests of thousands of BBC viewers who were annoyed and disappointed by the poor sound quality and the low mumbling of the actors in its TV period drama *Jamaica Inn*. She said 'Actors must remember who they're doing it for. They're doing for the audience. How can you be an actor if people can't understand what you're saying? Go and be Marcel Marceau [the mime artist] if you don't want people to understand you.' She further suggested that the prevailing trend of poor diction would be vastly improved by actors spending more time treading the boards. 'A lot of the mumbly actors should have a bash at Oscar Wilde or Noel Coward in the theatre, because if people can't hear what you're saying, they don't laugh and that would bring them up sharp.' I'm certain that Derek Newark would have said Amen to that.

Although he had completed his training and had joined the professional ranks, the people at RADA did not forget Derek, the former Guardsman and army officer. Early in 1972, the incumbent Principal invited him back to serve as a military consultant on the army play *Events While Guarding the Bofors Gun* by John McGrath, to be performed at the Vanbrugh Theatre. His advice was much valued and he was called upon again to work on the classic 1929 *Journey's End*, set in the trenches of the Great War. The Principal's rehearsal memorandum included this final paragraph:

> I am inviting Derek Newark, who always helps us with military plays, to give you some useful background information to the play [*Journey's End*]. He is going to talk about trench warfare, military discipline and procedure, etc. As an actor he knows exactly what will be of practical use for you to know. He will also give instruction on particular things such as the correct way of saluting. Be ready with questions as this will be the only occasion on which he will be with you. I'm sure you will find this first session of great value and interest.

CHAPTER 5
Nearly Drowned by Michael Winner

In 1961 Derek, aged 28, was raring to go. Backed by his vigorous agent Elizabeth Robinson, he was eager to experience every medium on offer: stage, films, television and radio. On graduating from RADA with a diploma, Derek applied for membership of Equity, the actors' union. He was granted full membership on 7 December 1960 and paid the first instalment of a guinea for the subscription of four guineas per annum. He was now a *bona fide* professional. He went immediately into his first commercial stage role, a small part in a drama about redbrick university life called *The Tinker*, written by Laurence Dobie and Robert Sloman.

A Bristol Old Vic production, it opened on 7 December 1960 at London's Comedy Theatre. Derek played Charlie, a regular at the students' pub run by Sam. He also understudied the lead character, Harry Brown, played by the rising star Edward Judd. Others in the cast (who would later become successful) included Richard Gale, Ewan Hooper, Terence Davies, Denis Chinnery, Stephanie Cole and Annette Crosbie.

The critics liked the play and Judd, as the working-class hero, was hailed as a new star in the making. Robert Muller of the *Daily Mail* said Judd's 'technique reminds one of the young Richard Burton'. The play was set for a decent run. Then, on 3 January 1961, Edward Judd suddenly collapsed after the first act. Derek was presented with a great opportunity. As the understudy, he stepped smoothly into the leading role and proved himself a minor success for the rest of the run, but there was more to Judd's sudden 'collapse' than met the eye.

Derek told me that three weeks into the play's run, Judd said to him 'Do yourself a favour, Newark, pay extra attention to my dialogue, 'cos I won't be around for much longer... I've got bigger fish to fry.'

Derek was somewhat baffled by this comment but took the advice to heart. He later discovered that Judd, poised on the springboard of cinematic stardom was secretly committed to a major movie and wanted an early exit from *The Tinker*. The film in question, in which Judd played a leading role, was the science-fiction movie *The Day the Earth Caught Fire*, shot in the UK in black-and-white and released in 1961.

Edward Judd went on the make several major films and was even seriously considered for the part of James Bond in *Dr No* (1962), but he never did realise his self-presumed Hollywood stardom. His twinkle soon faded. It was said that some influential directors found Judd—aka 'Big-ead'—difficult to deal with. His subsequent heavy drinking did not help his declining career. He continued working in films and TV in small parts and eventually became a voice-over merchant in TV commercials.

BANG OUT OF ORDER!

Despite being instrumental in giving Derek his first big break, I never took to Eddy Judd. On the several occasions I drank with him, I found the man a vain poseur, totally self-obsessed, and boastful to a boring degree. I remember one occasion when he walked into a Soho afternoon drinking club, in his middle fifties by then, a failed but still flickering film star. He posed in the doorway at the top of a short flight of stairs for a few spotlight minutes, then walked slowly to the bar. He was wearing denim jacket and jeans, white tee-shirt, cowboy boots, dark glasses, and a badly-fitting hairpiece—an ersatz edition of Paul Newman. He ended his days in a charity-run retirement home for actors and died in 2009, aged 76.

Taking over the lead in *The Tinker* proved a big boost to Derek's early endeavours and it led to regular work in television, which paid quite well compared to stage work. He got a small role in one episode of the TV adventure series *The Avengers*, starring Patrick Macnee and Honor Blackman—she of the tight leather cat-suit. Then as a customs man in ATV Network's *Probation Officer*, followed by another small part in ATV's *Harpers West One*, about life in a big department store. For a single episode in ATV's series *Deadline Midnight* in 1961, Derek was paid two guineas (two pounds two shillings) for rehearsal time and 30 guineas for his performance.

In May 1961, Derek received a letter from Pieter Rogers, general manager of the English Stage Company:

BANG OUT OF ORDER!

Dear Derek,
THE TRIPLE ALLIANCE by JA Cuddon.

We are very pleased that you have agreed to appear in Keith Johnstone's production of *The Triple Alliance*, to be presented by The English Stage Society at the Royal Court Theatre on Sunday May 28th 1961 at 7.30pm.

This is to confirm that the engagement includes a rehearsal period which commenced on Monday, May 15th, and that we will pay you a token expense allowance of £2.2s.

We very much hope that this production will prove personally successful for you, as well as for The English Stage Society.

The Triple Alliance was a pretentious one-night performance. The critic Robert Muller said of this dark, eristical essay 'A drama which reminds one in turn of Oedipus, Hammer Horrors, and John Arden is not designed to send one out into the May night whistling... the setting is a home for "cripples" and its chief characters are a hunchback, a club-foot, one man who cannot use his arms, and another who cannot walk.' Bamber Gascoigne in *The Spectator* had this to say of a very difficult play: 'At the start it was derivative, with some success, from Samuel Beckett. But by the end—when the cripples had gone off with a darkly supernatural window-cleaner... the play had become a parody of Eliot. The chief pleasure of the evening was Derek Newark's performance as the hunchback.' A far cry indeed from Jackie Styles.

In November 1961, Derek was based in Coventry. As a member of the Belgrade Theatre Company, his bourgeoning stagecraft was tested in a varied repertoire of new and established plays, both drama and comedy. The Company included a young Ian McKellen. In *You Never Can Tell* by George Bernard Shaw, Derek played Mr Bohun, QC. In *When We Are Married* by JB Priestly, he was the Rev Clement Mercer. In *The Seagull* by Chekhov, Derek had the role of Doctor Dorm. In *The Caretaker*, a three-handed drama by Harold Pinter, Derek played Mick. Starting on 13 November, the Company staged a double-bill for two weeks: *The Man in the Cage* by the new young writer Susan Hill, a short two-man essay in which Derek played Kerr; the main production being *Celebration*, a comedy by Keith Waterhouse and Willis Hall, with Derek as Jack Lucas, the bride's brother.

On 27 November came the new play *End of Conflict*, a military drama written by a fresh young talent named Barry England, in which Derek played the disturbed Private Varley and Ian McKellen as Lieutenant Simon Mason. The successful and busy season ended with Derek as Sam Weller in *Mr Pickwick* and as Chief Stoat in *Toad of Toad Hall*. *End of Conflict* was reviewed by *The Guardian*:

> This play by a young author, Barry England [an ex-officer], who has obviously drawn heavily on his experiences in Malaya and China in the post-Korea period... His theme would seem to be the head-on

collision of individuality and idealism of a young officer within the hard pattern of Army existence... The stage company serves him well, particularly Ian McKellen as the young subaltern [2nd Lt Mason]; Mark Eden [Lt Brash, MC], who understands individuality but cannot condone it; and Donald Magill as 'Pongo' Standing the professional major. But the finest acting is that of Derek Newark as a tough, mixed-up Private Varley, a remarkable study in the frustration of ignorance.

Eric Shorter said of the play: 'Anthony Richardson's swift, sharp production of an excellent cast led by Ian McKellen, Mark Eden and Derek Newark falls sufficiently into military line and Kenneth Bridgeman's flimsy sets are extremely serviceable as well as handsome. It makes a good racy evening. No mystery, no poetry, but plenty of simple theatrical punch.'

End of Conflict served Derek well in his early career, as indeed he served the drama very well. He reprised his emotionally demanding role as Private Varley in a TV production shown on Channel Nine on 23 July 1963. The play is set in an army barracks in the Far East in the early 1950s. Its theme is a critique of the army's structured, disciplined way of life. Defence of the system—'It may not be perfect—what system is?—but it exists because it works'—is voiced by Acting-Adjutant Brash, played by Michael Atkinson. He's hard but fair and intelligent enough to understand both sides of the question—in answer to the provocative new arrival in the officers' mess. The arrogant new boy is a National Serviceman and intellectual snob, Second-Lieutenant Simon Mason, played by Barry Justice. His attempts as a 'part-time' soldier to impose his own idealistic methods on the system, while bypassing existing procedures, quickly antagonises his fellow officers. The ensuing 'end of conflict' comes with Mason's treatment of Private Varley, a difficult and regular offender he tries to help, that brings violent repercussions in its wake. It was a strong, emotional part for Derek, as Varley the simple, uneducated private soldier enmeshed in a situation he doesn't fully understand.

At this point of his early progress Derek was enthralled by classical theatre. As a member of The Royal Shakespeare Company, he appeared in Bertolt Brecht's *The Caucasian Chalk Circle* at London's Aldwych Theatre in May 1962. It was during the latter production that Derek nearly throttled the leading actor, Hugh Griffith. It happened in the 'hanging' scene in act two. Derek played one of three Iron Troopers who, according to the play, pretended to hang Azdac the Judge (Griffith) in order to frighten him. Azdac stood on a box with a noose around his neck and Derek pulled the rope taut. He would then quickly release it. But Griffith slipped off the rickety box and the stage joke nearly became a real tragedy—the noose tightened around his throat and he blacked out. The curtain was rung down and he was carried from the stage unconscious.

Some 15 minutes later, revived by a stiff brandy the actor returned to carry on. But it had been a close call. The *London Evening Standard* reported Derek explaining his part in the incident: 'If I hadn't let go of the rope it would have been disaster. Mr Griffith fell over towards me. I went to grip him and when he fell he was underneath me.'

The next classical 'scalp' on Derek's theatrical belt was

Beckett's *Waiting for Godot*, staged during a season at the Nottingham Playhouse in November 1962, in which he had the challenging role of Pozzo. 'Blustering and ever alert for one-upmanship,' noted the *Nottingham Evening Post*, 'Derek Newark's Pozzo is massive and commanding; even his blind Pozzo is like a stranded whale.' The Nottingham season included *The Three Musketeers* by Dumas. Derek played Porthos, Daniel Massey was Athos and Richard Hampton, Aramis. D'Artagnan was played by the handsome John Neville, who later rose to theatrical heights. The cast also fielded the competent Terence Rigby.

'Those swashbuckling Three Musketeers flash their swords at the Playhouse for the next three weeks when a new translation of the famous story opens on Tuesday,' reported the *Nottingham Evening Post*. 'Forty-five roles will be doubled by 22 players, and at one point there will be 15 people fighting in spectacular swordplay so hectic that St John's Ambulance men will be standing by in case someone gets too enthusiastic. Already several actors have sustained cuts in the fight sequences worked out by actors Derek Newark and Roger Jerome, both expert fencers.'

In a busy 1962, Derek appeared at the Theatre Royal Windsor in a drama called *Red on White* written by the Canadian-born actor Alexander Knox, a familiar face in British and American feature films. The play's action takes place in a holiday cabin in the far northwest of Canada. Its leading man was a tall, young, promising Canadian named Donald Sutherland, then living in England, and Derek Newark played Sergeant Parcy, a red-coated Mounted Policeman. Sutherland, like Derek, was an alumnus of RADA. In 1963, Derek was strutting his stuff with the Royal Shakespeare Company in a short run of *As You Like It*. This production had a stellar cast including Ian Bannen, Vanessa Redgrave, Patrick Wymark, Roy Dotrice, Max Adrian, Russell Hunter, Patsy Byrne, and Gordon Costelow.

Following his intense performance as a disturbed soldier in the 1963 television production of the army drama *End of Conflict*, Derek began to get an increasing amount of TV and film work. Both mediums paid better that stage productions. But he still found time to tread the boards. He loved the rapport between actor and audience, the immediate reaction of a packed house to the dialogue, gestures and jokes of the players, and, of course, the beloved sound of applause. In September 1964, he was fully occupied at the Queens Theatre, Hornchurch, in Essex, not far from Derek's family home in Romford.

He was cast in *Chips With Everything*, a drama set in an RAF station, written by the successful Arnold Wesker of the then fashionable 'kitchen-sink' school of playwrights. The action concerned the progress of a batch of nine National Service recruits arriving for their basic training who are seen on the drill square, at bayonet practice, and eating in the Naafi canteen, hence the working-class habit of eating chips with every meal. Derek was well cast as Corporal Hill the drill instructor. It's interesting to note that the part of Recruit 276 'Pip' Thompson was played by a promising young thespian named Edward Fox.

From a professional viewpoint, Derek always regarded Edward as a better actor than his younger brother James Fox, who was at that time a burgeoning film star, having made a big impact in the 1963 film *The Servant*. Derek would meet up a number of times with Edward over the coming years, on TV productions and on movie sets. Both would appear in the films *Oh! What a Lovely War* (1969) and *The Breaking of Bumbo* (1970). Nine years after *Chips With Everything*, Edward Fox became an international star playing the assassin in *Day of the Jackal*.

Chips ran for two weeks at the Queens, followed by *The Doctor and the Devils* by Dylan Thomas, in which Derek played Dr Robert Knox, a real-life Scottish anatomist who became involved with the notorious 'body-snatchers' Burke and Hare. In need of a constant supply of fresh cadavers for dissection, Knox hired the services of William Burke and William Hare to provide the required bodies. But unknown to Knox they did not rob the graves of the newly buried, they supplied cadavers by murder. To save himself from execution, Hare turned King's Evidence against Burke, who was hanged in 1829. Derek managed to convince with a decent enough Edinburgh accent. He told me he played the part with Tod Slaughter in mind, a much watered-down version of the old master of melodrama who died in 1956.

*****

Over the next few years, with his growing skill, and the aid of his able agent Elizabeth Robinson, Derek was busy in TV series and in feature films. He made good money and moved from his Romford flat to a big Victorian house in Purley, near Croydon. In November 1963, Derek appeared in BBC television's new children's show *Doctor Who*, starring William Hartnell, which later developed into the phenomenal, world's longest-running sci-fi serial. Derek was in the very first episode called *An Unearthly Child*, cast as a caveman; his cave-dwelling buddy being the well-known actor Howard Lang. The hairy cavemen were short on dialogue but big on grunts and impressive gestures. The female producer of the groundbreaking show, Verity Lambert, sent Derek the following note:

> Dear Derek,
> Just a note to thank you very much for all the work you put in on our first serial of Dr Who. It was a great pleasure working with you and I hope that we will have the opportunity to do so again in the future.

In between his numerous TV appearances, Derek was making his way into the movie world. In 1963, he had a small part as a rugby player in *This Sporting Life*, starring Richard Harris and Rachel Roberts. It was director Lindsay Anderson's first feature film, which also included in its cast, William Hartnell (famous as Dr Who) and Arthur Lowe (who later became Captain Mainwaring in *Dad's Army*). In the same year, Derek was filming in a Michael Winner production called *The System* (released in 1964). He played Alfred, a tough guy rival of the leading man, Oliver Reed. The film, a romantic drama of young love in modern Britain, was written by Peter Draper, photographed in black-and-white by Nicolas Roeg, and directed on a very tight budget by Winner, then aged 27. Prominent members of the cast were Jane Merrow, Julia Foster, Harry Andrews, John Alderton, and David Hemmings.

Winner, a Cambridge University prodigy, was an ebullient and precocious talent who had produced and directed his first film at the age of 22. He was notorious in the film business for paying his cast of minor actors the bare minimum; even the principal players received less than top rates. Importantly, he scrooged on hiring stuntmen. From the start of his long career, Winner seemed to model himself on Eric Von Stroheim, the legendary Austrian actor and despotic director of many Hollywood epics. When asked for his definition of making a film, Winner replied: 'Well, it's really a team effort—a lot of people doing exactly what I say.'

Derek didn't take easily to Winner's overbearing, single-minded style of direction and made his feelings known. Winner was adamantine about what he wanted on screen and would instruct his actors accordingly in his usual forthright manner. He might consult his principals, or star, but never the small-part players. Winner left no doubt who was boss on set. Derek formed the impression that Winner didn't warm to him, and that the parsimonious young director put him in unnecessary physical harm because he would not use—or did not want to pay for—a professional stuntman. Now Derek, aged 30, prided himself on his physical capabilities and courage. He had already done a rough-and-tumble sequence himself, which involved falling down a short staircase, for 'no extra pay', but the next time Winner called upon him for additional stunt action, he demurred. Winner insisted.

'Come on, Derek, I want you to do it for authenticity. You're a fit young man. We don't need a body double for this little shot. It's a simple stunt. Nothing can go wrong. Right... let's do it!'

The sequence involved Derek being thrown into Folkstone harbour in what he assessed to be a deep and dangerous situation, plunging in between a moving camera-boat and the harbour wall. Derek was not a good swimmer. He could foresee the possible peril. It really was a stuntman's task. But Derek's growing reputation as a hard man actor was in question. He imagined the gossip on the set.

'Did you hear... Derek Newark lost his bottle.'

It was white feather time.

'That mean bastard Winner gave me no choice. Against my better judgement I agreed.'

Derek was thrown bodily into the brackish water. The camera-boat moved in close to take the shot. Derek came up gasping and thrashing, and they pulled him out. It seemed good enough, but Winner wasn't happy with the take.

'Let's do it again!'

After the third and final time of being tossed into the cold sea, Derek formed the unkind opinion that 'Winner was having a go at me... his sneaky way of telling me who was boss.' Derek told me that during the incident he had a terrible flashback to his infancy when he nearly drowned in the boating-pond at Great Yarmouth.

Later that day, when the cast and crew were eating at the ad hoc canteen, Derek, sitting with the camera-crew, was relaxed and relieved after his soaking. He was, perhaps, laughing and joking and talking too loudly for some people's comfort. The moody Oliver Reed, sitting quietly with another group, suddenly shouted: 'Why don't you shut up, Newark!'

All went silent.

Then Derek stood up, defiantly, and threw down the gauntlet. 'Why don't you make me?'

The robust leading man did not rise to the customary bait. He remained seated and calmly replied: 'Fuck off, Newark. Go to hell.'

'I'm already there,' jeered Derek, 'working for Winner!'

The cheeky retort raised laughter from almost everybody within earshot, but Oliver Reed was a favourite at the court of 'Prince' Michael and Derek never worked for Winner again.

In 1964, Derek appeared as the Mess Sergeant in the *Redcap* TV series starring John Thaw as a military policeman. In October, Derek played Private Postnikov, a Russian soldier in the BBC TV drama *A Crack in the Ice*. Lyn Lockwood of the *Daily Telegraph* reviewed it:

> All Private Postnikov did was desert his sentry-post to save a drunken peasant, who had fallen through a hole in the ice. Guilty of being a human being you might say. But there is no room for human beings in a world where the State is everything. So the wretched soldier found himself being ground in the cogs of the machine. There were several excellent passages [in this play] last night. But the experimental technique used by Ronald Eyre, who adapted a short story by the 19th-century Russian writer Nikolai Leskov, was somewhat cumbersome... leaving nothing in the satirical comedy-drama to the imagination. The story, one felt, could have been told more effectively without the self-conscious display of techniques. Bill Fraser, James Maxwell, Michael Horden, and Derek Newark gave good performances.

The following New Year brought Derek considerable benefit in television terms when he was chosen as a regular character in the fictional Fleet Street newspaper series *Front Page Story*, created by Wilfred Greatorex, a former journalist. Derek played Joe Harwood, a thorough, direct, dogged man who hammers on doors where Danny Tarrant, his colleague, would nip in round the back. Derek shared top billing with Derek Godfrey who played Danny Tarrant. The first episode called *The Runaways* was scripted by Keith Dewhurst, who would later feature largely in Derek's stage career at the National Theatre, and was shown on ATV Network at prime time on 2 February 1965.

It proved a busy and lucrative year. In August he went on location to the Republic of Ireland to film *The Blue Max*, a mega-budget Hollywood production about German flying aces of the First World War. Top of the cast were the American George Peppard as German ace Bruno Stachel, James Mason as Count von Klugermann, and Ursula Andress as Countess Kaeti. Supporting actors playing German airmen included the British actors Jeremy Kemp, Harry Towb, Derren Nesbitt, and Derek Newark as Ziegel the squadron's chief mechanic. The German Carl Schell played the 'Red Baron' von Richtofen. The flying scenes were mostly shot on an old airfield near Dublin. The Battle of the Somme was re-created in Wicklow County, 30 miles south of Dublin, and a thousand soldiers of the Irish Army were employed in the realistic combat scenes.

The aerial sequences and dogfights staged in *The Blue Max* were truly spectacular. The aircraft featured were meticulous replicas reconstructed by experts for the film. Chief among the German planes was the Fokker Triplane, a single-seat scout with three wings, armed with twin machine-guns mounted forward of the pilot and synchronised to fire through the propeller. Baron von Richtofen and his squadron flew the Fokker. The Baron's triplane was painted all red to distinguish his mount from the others, like a medieval knight. George Peppard, already an experienced pilot, took an intensive flying course to add 210 hours on his log, 130 of them solo. On location in Ireland he spent an additional month flying the replica aircraft.

Derek was impressed by Peppard, by his movie career and by his persona. He cultivated his friendship, drinking and chatting about acting and life in general. Both had served in the army: Peppard had joined the US Marines at the age of 17. April Ashley, the actress and Peppard's new wife who had accompanied him to Ireland, referred to her husband as 'Perfect George' because everything about him had to be perfect: his teeth, his blond hair, his film uniform, his normal clothes, his shoes, his speech, his manners. Derek noted that 'Even the hairs on the back of his head were perfect.'

At that time, Peppard's film career was in full flight. Everything was going perfectly for 'Perfect George'. After a successful television period in the 1950s, he appeared in ever-bigger parts in major movies: as Corporal Chuck Fedderson in *Pork Chop Hill* (1959); as Rafe Copley, Robert Mitchum's illegitimate son, in *Home From The Hill* (1960). He narrowly lost out in the casting lottery of that classic Western *The Magnificent Seven* (1960). He had been first choice to play the enigmatic character Vin... but a virtually unknown actor got the part—Steve McQueen; it made him an international star.

George, however, struck Hollywood gold himself by landing the star-making role of Paul Varjak opposite Audrey Hepburn in *Breakfast at Tiffany's* (1961) that firmly established him as leading man material. The film was a huge box-office success and Peppard was suddenly in great demand. Between *Breakfast at Tiffany's* and *The Blue Max* he starred in five major movies, including *How The West Was Won* (1962), *The Victors* (1963), and *The Carpetbaggers* (1964), on the set of which he met his second wife Elizabeth Ashley. So, by the time the ambitious Derek Newark came into Peppard's dazzling orbit 'Perfect George' was an imposing celebrity, a star of proven value, a 'bankable' asset in Hollywood vernacular

It's not surprising that Derek was somewhat star-struck. He wanted to be Peppard's pal; he envied his perfect persona and cinematic success, the man who had kissed the delectable Audrey Hepburn! Peppard was well aware of his own growing stature. He held himself in high esteem; humility was an alien virtue. He viewed himself as a far superior person to most of the 'suckers' he came in contact with. Indeed, he was blessed in many ways: conventionally handsome with blond hair, six feet tall, athletic in build, good at sports, tennis, horsemanship, flying aircraft and racing cars. But Peppard was not as perfect as he appeared. He had serious character flaws that would prove deleterious in his burgeoning career: he developed an early alcoholic problem and his ego inflated to a destructive degree.

In his desire to be close to Peppard, the susceptible Derek allowed himself to be seduced into a game of poker with the arrogant star. Derek knew the rudiments of the game but was never a regular player. He made this clear to Peppard, who suspiciously replied, 'You wouldn't be trying to hustle me, would you Derek?' Meaning, you wouldn't be trying to bamboozle or mislead me. So Derek reluctantly agreed to play the role of sucker.

When they sat down to play, Derek described to me in detail how Peppard immediately transformed himself into the mode of Mississippi riverboat gambler: green eyeshade capped an immobile face, cigar in mouth, a glass of bourbon to hand; his immaculate fingers manipulating the cards with practiced dexterity. Peppard was soon aware that Derek was not a hustler, that he was not a worthy adversary; but Peppard's all-conquering ego knew no mercy, no moral boundary, he had to be the winner, the best, no doubt about it. Fortunately for Derek, little money was at stake.

At the end of the one-sided game, Derek was neither humbled by the unfair experience nor was his competitive spirit subdued. He cheerfully proposed that they play squash at the soonest opportunity and the triumphant gambler readily agreed, for he considered himself to be an all-round sportsman. Derek excelled at aggressive physical sports as opposed to cerebral disciplines such as card games or chess. He enjoyed the contact violence of rugby and football, fencing and judo, tennis and squash.

On the squash court, George was superbly turned-out in pristine whites, shirt, shorts, socks and gymshoes—the very picture of a perfect model for sportswear. Derek a regular gladiator in the squash arena was dressed in grubby old sweatshirt and shorts. Squash is a racket game played with a soft rubber ball in a closed wall court. It's a tough, unrelenting contest of non-stop physical confrontation and endurance.

'I was 32, more than match fit,' Derek told me, 'and utterly determined to knock the swank out of that arrogant Yank.'

It seemed that his admiration for Peppard was slowly evaporating. George was five years older than Derek; he was a heavy cigarette smoker with an alcohol problem... but his ego was big, powerful and healthy. He put up a decent enough early effort, but Derek ran him ragged. George couldn't equal his overwhelming energy and endurance and eventually cried off with 'excruciating' leg cramp. It was, after all, a private affair, no audience to witness his discomfit. Derek did not exalt in his silent victory. He had proved his superiority in his chosen sport and decided to be magnanimous.

'Toughest set I've had in a long time. Well played George... let's do it again sometime.' The now not-so-perfect George, somewhat crestfallen, his brilliant whites now soaked dark with sweat, did not take up the offer of a rematch.

Peppard's subsequent career is an interesting example of the ups-and-downs of a one-time golden boy in the movie business. After *The Blue Max*, he made 11 feature films, all of them forgettable. He became notorious among producers and directors as a prima donna, being conceited and awkward, difficult to work with, never knowing when to keep his mouth shut. He was cast in the lead of *Sands of the Kalahari* (1965) but had an early difference of opinion with the director Cy Enfield and walked out of the picture after only a few days shooting. His disputatious demeanour lost him the plum role of Blake Carrington in the TV drama series *Dynasty*, that became an amazing global success. He was fired after just three weeks wrangling on the set and replaced with the lesser well known but dependable John Forsythe who became the permanent star, and international celebrity, of the long-running show.

Peppard's career was in the doldrums when providence dealt the poker-playing George a good hand. He landed the lead in a TV series called *Banacek*, as the eponymous private eye Thomas Banacek, an urbane character of Polish descent. The show proved popular, especially so with the Polish-American public; a people who had long suffered—like the Irish—as butts of 'Polack' jokes depicting them as dense and slow-witted. At last they had a TV hero to be proud of, a wealthy Boston private eye, clever, elegant and articulate, who cruised around in a chauffeur-driven limousine, delivering justice salted with pithy Polish proverbs. This successful show ran for two years, ending in September 1974.

Banacek was followed by a lacuna in his acting career. He was too closely identified with the part. So he tried his untested abilities as producer and director, but to little avail. Truth was, he was only good as an actor. Then destiny once again dealt him an excellent hand and he kept his trap shut and made the most of it. He revelled in the tongue-in-cheek role of Colonel John 'Hannibal' Smith, the swaggering, cigar-chomping, gun-toting leader of a maverick commando unit in the TV adventure series *The A-Team*, which ran from 1983 to 1987. He was so popular that in 1985 he was awarded a pavement star on the tourist Walk of Fame on Hollywood Boulevard.

Time, however, was fast running out for George Peppard. His last acting job came in March 1994, a supporting role in an episode of the TV series *Matlock*. He had managed to overcome his serious drinking habit in 1978 and spent his later years helping other alcoholics. He had smoked three packs of cigarettes a day for most of his life and quit the addiction when diagnosed with lung cancer in 1992 and had part of his lung removed. He died of pneumonia in May 1994, aged 65. He was married five times and had three children

On a couple of soul-searching occasions, he said of himself: 'I was my own worst enemy in my drinking days... My life hasn't been a string of victories. It's no golden past. I am no George Peppard fan.'

During the making of *The Blue Max*, Derek met up with an ex-army officer friend, Derek Agutter (father of Jenny Agutter), with whom he had served in Singapore. Agutter was working on the production side of the film and he later became head of Combined Services Entertainment and Derek helped him out during a tight period by handling a couple of shows on tour. Derek became friendly with several other cast members, some he had worked with before in TV, and some he would work with in future TV, films and stage: Jeremy Kemp from the police series *Z-Cars*; Harry Towb, a familiar face on TV, Peter Woodthorpe, and Derren Nesbitt who played fighter pilot Fabian in *The Blue Max*.

Derek viewed Nesbitt as somewhat of a rival in the business. They both looked similar in their *Spotlight* photographs—the actors' casting book. Both had trained at RADA (Nesbitt was two years younger than Derek); both would work for Peter Hall, and both appeared in the same numerous TV series. Although Nesbitt had achieved acclaim at RADA, winning the prestigious Forbes-Robertson Shakespeare Acting and Kendal Award, Derek was firmly convinced that he was the better actor of the two. And he was right. Nesbitt was more the leading-man type, whereas Derek was the versatile protean character actor. Nevertheless, Nesbitt was very successful in supporting roles in TV and films, often vying for the same parts.

In *The Blue Max*, both Derek and Derren had much larger parts in the shooting script and they naturally had expected to see some good personal close-ups and action sequences up on the big screen, but the editor ruthlessly cut their exposure in favour of more of the star principals, and therefore greatly diminished the supporting roles of Derek and Derren. Derek in particular described to me one exciting sequence where he rushes to the rescue, pulling a pilot from a burning plane, a good action piece that never reached the screen. And several expressive close-ups were also left on the cutting-room floor as redundant to the finished product.

The Blue Max was released in 1966 and proved a box-office success. In the year 1965, Derek told me that he had earned, from TV and film, a total of £10,000, most of which being his fee for *The Blue Max*. The big pay-cheque enabled Derek to move his family from their modest Romford flat in Essex to a large detached house at Purley, Surrey. The world looked good to Derek, promising TV, film and stage star.

CHAPTER 6
Brecht and Boozing

On his return from Ireland filming *The Blue Max*, having worked and mixed socially with Hollywood film stars, Derek continued his jobbing television roles: two episodes of the cop show *Softly Softly*, and three episodes of *The Baron*. In November 1966, he donned the mantle of Arthur Clegg, a gamekeeper, in the Rediffusion Network production of *The Hunting of Aubrey Hopkins*, starring Roy Dotrice, an episode in the *Blackmail* drama series. In between TV and films, Derek went on tour in April 1966 with Bob Monkhouse in *Roman Candle*, a new comedy by Sidney Sheldon, in which he played Sergeant Eddie Woods. He got on so well with Monkhouse that in the same year he appeared with him in the Rodgers and Hart musical comedy *The Boys from Syracuse*.

In January 1967, Derek was interviewed by John Newnham for the *Eastern Evening News*:

> It seems impossible to avoid seeing Yarmouth-born Derek Newark on the film and TV screens these days. Derek is the actor who first attracted TV attention as ace reporter Joe Harwood in the *Front Page Story* series. You

may have seen him recently in the cinema as a German officer in *The Blue Max*, and during the past few months he doesn't seem to have been off the TV screens for more than a week or so at any time. He played a very funny, but realistic drunk in a recent episode of *The Likely Lads* ('Everyone said it was type-casting!' he cracked). He was a tough sergeant in a *Drama '67* play, *Conduct to the Prejudice* a few weeks ago, and he was the tough, murderous third mate in the two-part *The Baron* story *Storm Warning* which has just been shown. This week, he has been the smoothly intellectual villain in the first of the new *Avengers* episodes, and among his other appearances is that of a detective-constable in *Coronation Street*.

'It seems like tempting fate to say that I'm getting so many parts,' Derek said. 'I suppose I've been lucky in that, since *Front Page Story*, I haven't been stuck to one character. Villainy, I suppose, has predominated, but each character has been quite different from the others...

'One of the most difficult roles,' he confessed, 'was in a *Blackmail* episode. I was cast as a grotty Norfolk gamekeeper. It should have been easy, of course, since I was born in Norfolk [but raised in Essex] and people expect you to be able to conjure up a local accent. I found it tough going! Spent a lot of time with a Norfolk friend and he helped me to get the accent I've never had!'

BANG OUT OF ORDER!

A few months later, the stentorian Derek landed a barracuda of a character as the terrifying Sergeant Huber, a German drill-instructor in Kaiser Wilhelm's army of 1912. Adapted by John Hale from the DH Lawrence story *The Thorn in the Flesh* and screened by Granada Television in October 1967, it tells of a young conscript's ordeal in training under the harsh command of the martinet Huber. Martin Bachmann, the recruit, played by newcomer Michael Cadman, has a horror of heights and his nerve fails him on the 30-foot scaling ladder, with the fierce Huber standing at the top, shouting. When he accidentally strikes the sergeant, fear of reprisal makes him desert. He falls in love with the maid from the manor house who shelters him. Sylvia Clayton of the *Daily Telegraph* wrote in her review: 'Derek Newark was terrifying as Sergeant Huber with a voice loud enough to make a ladder tremble.' The *TV Times* reported some inside information to its readers:

> Was there really a slight chill in the air socially for Derek Newark? Or was it only imagination that he was alone more than usual on the three-days' location filming for *The Thorn in the Flesh*? Or had he, during the morning sessions so immersed himself in the character of Sergeant Huber that the others just didn't want to know him any more? 'Anyway,' said Derek, 'there was I in the evenings hard at it chatting up people to show I wasn't really like that.'

Michael Cadman just missed National Service, so to get the feel of the army, he and the rest of the squad volunteered for drill every morning before rehearsal. This is where Derek Newark's five years as a regular soldier came in useful. Derek, who had been in the Coldstream Guards, was given the task of drilling his fellow actors.

'I treated them as I thought Huber would have,' said Derek, 'and the effect was electrifying.' Michael Cadman took up the story: 'The drill put us in the right frame of mind. We all took it very seriously with Derek right in character yelling if we made a mistake.'

In the same month this was screened, Derek was back in the serious theatre in *The Public Prosecutor* staged at the Hampstead Theatre Club in October 1967. An obscure political play by the Bulgarian author Georgi Djagarov, it was adapted for an English audience by the husband-and-wife team of CP Snow and Pamela Hansford. The story is set in the bad old days of the Stalinist-Marxist government in communist Bulgaria. The action takes place in a provincial town between winter 1955 and spring 1956. The public prosecutor, Marko Voynov, was played by Glyn Owen; Derek was his brother Boyan. The audience and the critics found this abstruse drama heavy going. WA Darlington curtly ended his review in *The Telegraph* with: 'The piece was well received. The author was present and took a call.'

The rivalry between Derek and Derren Nesbitt culminated in the war film *Where Eagles Dare* in 1968. A Second World War action thriller based on a novel by Alistair MacLean, who also wrote the screenplay, *Where Eagles Dare* starred Richard Burton, Clint Eastwood, Mary Ure, and Patrick Wymark. When the producers were casting the minor parts both Derek Newark and Derren Nesbitt were considered for roles as German officers. Derek desired the part of SS Major von Hapen, a substantial cameo appearance in a major scene. Unfortunately for him, Nesbitt nabbed the role and made much use of this standout opportunity. Derek got the far lesser part of the officer leading his troops in a final shoot-out sequence with the heroes. As I remember it, Derek's minimal dialogue delivered while waving his Luger pistol, comprised of the exclamatory *'Schiessen! Schnell Feuer!'*

It was an all-action movie celebrated for the fight on the alpine cable car and the producers employed a battalion of stuntmen—so many in fact that Clint Eastwood dubbed the film 'Where Doubles Dare'. Richard Burton was paid a million dollars plus a percentage of what turned out to be a hugely profitable picture.

Derek's stand-out TV performance as Sergeant Huber caught the attention of Richard Attenborough, veteran actor now directing his first feature film, *Oh! What a Lovely War,* a satirical anti-war melange of songs, battles, and a few jokes. Attenborough, who was also co-producer with Brian Duffy, had signed-up some of the biggest names in show business, including Ralph Richardson, John Gielgud, Jack Hawkins, John Mills, three of the Redgrave family, Maggie Smith, Laurence Olivier, Susannah York, Dirk Bogarde, Phyllis Calvert, Kenneth More, and the promising Edward Fox and Derek Newark

Without such a stellar cast, Paramount would not have put up the 3½ million dollars needed to make the movie. Attenborough directed without a fee but would receive royalties if the film made a profit. Conversely, the big names played relatively small parts, generals and politicians in brief burlesque sequences. The key element, the eleven-strong Smith Family, played by minor actors, represented the 'common people' caught up in a disastrous war. The film was shot on location on the old Brighton pier and in the Brighton Pavilion, in a busy fairground environment. Derek played the Shooting Gallery Proprietor who hands out uniforms as prizes.

Based on Joan Littlewood's original low-budget stage production, the film lasts two hours 24 minutes. The sweeping closing sequence shows row upon row of white crosses—15,000 in total—covering a hillside, a poignant ending to an unusual and impressive film. *Oh! What a Lovely War* had its black-tie world premier at the Paramount Cinema in Piccadilly Circus on 10 April 1969 and Derek was there among the galaxy of stars and celebrities. The film was a critical success and set the seal on Richard Attenborough's future career as a prominent director. Some months later, in response to Derek's written note of congratulations on the film's success, Attenborough replied:

My Dear Derek, thank you so much for your kind letter. As you may well imagine, we were all tremendously thrilled to gain so many Awards... I hope you are doing well and that it will not be too long before we are working together again. Fondest regards, yours, [signed] Dickie A

*****

BANG OUT OF ORDER!

In August 1969 Derek's agent wrote him a letter saying, sadly, that she was leaving the theatre business completely, suggesting several other agents she thought would be most suitable. One of whom was Julia MacDermot, who recalls: 'When Liz Robinson was retiring she rang me to ask if I was interested in any of her clients and, without hesitation, I said Derek Newark, whose work I had seen and admired. In due course I met Derek, and for over an hour he had me in fits of laughter with little opportunity to discuss work.'

Derek went away to think about his future. After a bad experience with another transitory agent, he signed up with Julia in April 1971 for a probationary year at an agent's fee of 10% of all monies received. And to quote Julia again: 'So began many years of exasperation, rows, LOTS of laughter and enormous pride in seeing Derek's many brilliant performances.'

In November 1969, Derek was cast in a two-man play called *Staircase* at the Colchester Theatre in Essex. Written by veteran actor playwright Charles Dyer, this classic comedy drama examines the stormy relationship of two aging homosexual hairdressers. The stage set is a barber's shop in a south London back street. *Staircase* was first produced by Peter Hall at the Theatre Royal, Brighton, in 1966, and later at London's Aldwych Theatre with Paul Scofield scoring a huge personal success as the flamboyant Charles Dyer, 'Gawd help us all and Oscar Wilde!' Since then it has had many productions worldwide. At Nottingham, John Neville was acclaimed in the role created by Scofield. The film version saw Rex Harrison as Charles Dyer and Richard Burton as Harry Leeds. Both film stars were notorious womanisers and both were desperately miscast. Their 'camp' performance as the gay coiffeurs has been described as 'one of the silliest sights of the 1960s.'

The two-man *Staircase* was a difficult challenge for even the most accomplished of actors, so how did Derek, a relative newcomer to theatre-land, interpret the demanding role of Charlie Dyer? The review in the *Colchester Express* had this to say:

> Unlike the Burton-Harrison film, which to me was merely rather nasty, turgid and unpleasantly sordid, David Buxton's production underlines the sorry dilemma of its two half-life characters with humour, subtlety and telling silence. Derek Newark makes a blinding debut on his first appearance here with a savage petulance and frustration that renders his blatant vocabulary and phraseology as wounding as it is hilarious in a superb study, judged to the nth degree of audience reaction in its strength and skill of projection. John Harwood's pathetically domesticated Harry is an equally fine performance...

Local reviewer Seley Little recorded that:

> Colchester Repertory Company's production of this entirely contemporary minor masterpiece is little short of staggering—a team success that shines brilliantly and unforgettably, in every department. David Buxton's direction penetrates to the heart of a deep and expertly developed script, coaxing playing of the utmost responsiveness from both his heavily burdened actors.

> BANG OUT OF ORDER!
>
> In a splendid local debut Derek Newark precisely controls the show-biz camp element in Charlie, so that his highly involved playing is allowed to be a great deal more than a performance. John Harwood's stunned, aggrieved, proud and fussy little Harry is, likewise, an extraordinarily moving creation throughout.

Derek was now about to enter his most fertile phase as a theatrical actor, but it was also to be the moment when his consumption of alcohol would start to become a defining factor in his life and career. In private company he was indeed funny and entertaining, the ideal drinking companion... up to a point, a critical point. For there was another, a much darker side to Derek, and alcohol proved to be the liquid key that set free his dormant, drunken, dislikeable other self.

There are friends and associates who will say, and have said so in the past, that the Derek they knew was a kind and sensitive soul, generous in nature and help, sentimental and considerate, and that they never experienced a word or an action out of order. Well, that's as maybe, but I find it difficult to recognise that perfect Derek as the much-flawed brother that I came to know in later years. I knew Derek intimately all his life and I rarely, if ever, noted or enjoyed the generous virtues mentioned above, especially in his successful adult years.

As a close sibling, I mostly knew him to be sanctimonious when it suited him, sardonic and dismissive when it pleased him, truculent and disingenuous in argument and dissent. More bully than benevolent brother. It seemed to me that he regarded his siblings as family rivals, but with little or no talent or ambition. He was the top dog, the golden boy of the Newark trio, the presumed winner of three runners. Yes, he was the favourite, born to entertain. Yes, he was first out of the starting gates... but then he faded away as a loser in the great race of life. To quote from a show business song that Derek liked to sing: *It's Not How You Start—But How You Finish.*

Having listed all these negative elements about him, I have to confess in all honesty that I still miss him after all these years, miss him greatly. At his best he could be the funniest guy alive, a joy to be with. At his worst he was a foul-mouthed boorish braggart, aggressive and tiresome. Yes, there were violent and angry moments between us, but there again we had some wonderful times together. So when did his persona change from moderate social drinker to benighted boozer? In which period, at what time did his growing desire for evermore liquor reach tipping point?

As far as I can recall, his latent alcoholism had its genesis in the early 1970s when he joined the rowdy company of experimental actors, writers, and directors at London's Royal Court Theatre in Sloane Square. Here he came into sharp contention with a hungry pack of young, ambitious, and talented personalities, mostly from working-class and leftwing backgrounds, without dramatic training. They considered themselves natural performers, just right for the 'kitchen-sink' theatre popular at the time. Derek, an advocate of Conservative politics, a former Army officer, and RADA trained, was something of an oddball in this proletariat brigade of players. But by dint of hard work and hard drinking he made his considerable presence felt and became a worthy retainer at the Royal Court.

Bill Bryden, then an assistant-director at the Royal Court, took a shine to the industrious and reliable Derek and they became drinking mates, sharing dreams and plans of future projects and plays. To be called a Royal Court actor at that time was considered a theatrical accolade, and Derek's colleagues included many names and faces that were later to become famous on TV and in films: Bob Hoskins, Timothy Dalton, Robert Powell, Tim Curry, Henry Woolfe, Mark McManus, Brian Glover, Jack Shepherd, Patrick O'Connell, Kenneth Cranham, Trevor Peacock, Barrie Rutter, Dave Hill, Norman Beaton, the singer Georgia Brown, and the playwright Keith Dewhurst.

In conjunction with his ensemble years at the Royal Court, Derek was carving out a lucrative career in television and films, both mediums paying much more than stage work. With his rising income and public celebrity came a consequential rise in his consumption of hard liquor. Beer was never his cup of true joy. Vodka was his preferred choice of slow poison—vodka and tonic sans ice and lemon. I well remember once, when he made the point, 'And no lemon!' loud and clear to the barmaid, the cheeky girl pointed at me and said to Derek, 'Well, you brought him in'. When in a dark and belligerent mood he would imbibe brandy and soda... and woe betide anybody who would gainsay his opinions.

Our father, George senior, was also a hard drinker who enjoyed his pint of bitter beer, often followed by a whisky chaser. He was not an alcoholic in the clinical sense. He did not require or need a shot of liquor first thing in the morning to get him going, and he never drank at work. He was a binge drinker. Dad could go for several days, even weeks, without a drop of booze. Then, when the inevitable dark mood took him, he would fabricate an argument with mum, put on his Sunday suit, push in his false teeth, and march out of the house intent on getting thoroughly pissed. On his late and dreaded return he would create mayhem, shouting and cursing at mum and upsetting his anxious sons. Like Derek, dad was an ugly drunk.

*****

It was Derek's growing reputation as a player that drew him to the notice of Bill Bryden, a brilliant young Scottish director then working at London's Royal Court Theatre. And so, Derek became involved in the ill-conceived and ill-fated production that was *Pirates*, staged at The Theatre Upstairs, a kind of experimental cockpit, at the Royal Court on Sunday 13 December 1970 for one night only. Written by Keith Dewhurst and directed by Bill Bryden, it was succinctly described in the programme as 'a production without décor', meaning the entire action on board ship—with no ship—actually took place on a naked stage with a white outline of the ship's prow marked out on the stage floor.

It was the first of a series of 'impossible plays' staged at The Theatre Upstairs and continued later at the small Cottesloe space at the National Theatre. 'Impossible' in the sense that the wide scope and epic vision of the written piece far exceeded the props, space, and budget available to the limited area at the Court. And so it proved with *Pirates*. The actors were each paid the nominal fee of five pounds for a month's rehearsal and the one performance; the playwright received ten pounds.

BANG OUT OF ORDER!

Despite its talented cast that included Robert Powell, Patrick O'Connell, John Bennett, Brian Glover, Jack Shepherd, Norman Beaton, and Derek Newark, it was, in my humble opinion, the most boring, tedious theatre experience of my life. Too much wind, not enough sail. Too much sub-Elizabethan dialogue, not enough emotion or drama. The press reviews were lukewarm. It was a single Sunday night performance. The play sank without trace, never—as far as I'm aware—to be staged again. Nevertheless, Bill Bryden considered it a successful, noble experiment. He wrote to Derek:

> Well, the struggle is over. I feel absolutely shattered but I must take time to thank you for your hard and talented work that got *Pirates* ok and made it a success with the audience. I hope we work together again in the near future. If any of my plans come to fruition it should be soon...

He next worked with Bill Bryden at The Theatre Upstairs at the Royal Court in February 1971 in *The Baby Elephant* by Bertold Brecht. In the programme, Bryden found it necessary to personally justify his unusual presentation.

> A Bit of Explanation: We began work on this show as a kind of 'trailer' to our forthcoming production of Brecht's *Man is Man*, but things turned out somewhat differently. Brecht intended that *Baby Elephant* should be played in the foyer during the interval of a performance of *Man is Man*. By deciding to do it on its own, we found we had to put it in a different context. This led to experiment

and improvisation around the way the young Brecht was thinking in 1926, while working on the main play. This led to the mad collage about to be presented. It has little to do with *Man is Man* but quite a lot to do with what Brecht called 'smoker's theatre', a theatre in which the audience could relax. So you may smoke and you can drink (the bar's at the back). We hope you can relax and join in.

The Baby Elephant was a light-hearted satirical playlet on the British Army in India during the years of the Raj. It opened on 10 February, a curtain raiser to *Man is Man* that followed on 1 March. Derek played Sergeant Townley. The cast included Mark McManus, David Hill, Antony Milner, Tim Curry, and Bob Hoskins. Georgia Brown sang during the interlude. Brecht's German dialogue was translated by John Willnett and Bill Bryden directed. The leading critics delivered mixed reviews on *The Baby Elephant*, and later on *Man is Man*. The venerable Harold Hobson of *The Sunday Times* found it a 'curate's egg' of a play, that is, good in parts:

> The actors... are so confident and masterful that if [the playlet] is a trifle, it is a trifle of major proportions. The players are extremely accomplished. They move from outrageous burlesque to the most unexpected seriousness with absolute certainty...When the curtain fell there was no applause until a resourceful member of the cast broke the sombre hush with the words 'They're clapping!' in exactly the right tone of wonder and surprise.

BANG OUT OF ORDER!

Critic Irving Wardle wrote:

The Baby Elephant is a short extravaganza on the incidents and characters of *Man is Man*, written to be played as a side-show to the parent piece... however, it seems to have struck the company not only that *The Baby Elephant* was too brief to make an evening, but that it was a pretty terrible work on any terms... Bill Bryden's company is made up of the nucleus of the Ken Campbell Road Show. And entrusting Brecht to them is like engaging the Marx Brothers to celebrate Ella Wheeler Wilcox. They are not strong on cultural reverence; and they seem to have taken with relish to *The Baby Elephant* because they thought it a stinker... But they do get into their stride when a thunderous Sergeant, Derek Newark, takes over to drill them in the facts of Brecht's career as if he was explaining a weapon. The point is clearly and comically made against the figure of Brecht the boss; the cultural commissar who is [supposedly] beyond criticism.

Man is Man opened at the Royal Court Theatre on 1 March 1971. In the programme it was described as a 'comedy with songs by Bertolt Brecht. The metamorphosis of the packer Galy Gay in the military barracks at Kilkoa in the year 1925.' Translated by Steve Gooch, it was directed by William Gaskill assisted by Bill Bryden. The cast was composed of Henry Woolf as Galy Gay, Susan Williamson as his wife; Derek Newark as Jesse Mahoney, one of four soldiers in a machine-gun section, the other three being Barrie Rutter, Oliver Cotton, and Bob Hoskins. Georgia Brown played Widow Begwick, the singing canteen owner. It further presented the usual Brechtian satire on clownish and inhuman British soldiery.

Ronald Bryden in *The Observer* extolled Brecht as 'the greatest modern German poet. Among his plays Man is Man must be one of the least regarding in political wisdom, but it is an amazing poetic creation.' In the play, three soldiers kidnap the packer Galy Gay to take the place of a comrade wounded robbing a temple. By bribery and brainwashing they remake his identity, burying the personality of Galy Gay in a coffin over which he speaks the funeral oration. By the end he has become the perfect fighting automaton: a number in a file, happily killing in return for his food ration.

Derek did his usual research into Brecht's career as playwright and poet, but dug very little into his private and political life. Derek would deliver several pompous mini-lectures to me about the towering influence and wisdom of the German in the modern theatre. Despite Derek's proselytising, I did not, and never have, admired the Marxist chameleon that was Bertolt Brecht. He may have been a brilliant writer, but he was a poor example of a private person. An early Marxist, he became an exponent of communism and, with the rise of Nazism he fled Germany and sought asylum in Denmark, Sweden, Finland, and from 1941 to 1947, the United States, where he lived and worked in Hollywood.

Despite hating the American democratic social system, Brecht readily accepted the Yankee dollar. A life-long opponent of capitalist exploitation he once stated 'What is robbing a bank compared to founding one.' But this hypocritical Marxist was pragmatist enough to secure his fortune in a Swiss bank account. He returned to his homeland after the war and, welcomed by the repressive East German Government, was given a theatre and used as a communist cats-paw. During the 1953 uprising crushed by Soviet tanks, Brecht remained silent and inactive while brave protesters were killed in the streets outside his window. Thus, I was pleased to read the review by Felix Barker of *Man is Man*:

> All the solemn carry-on about Brecht simply has to be subjected to some sort of analysis. For ten years, we are told, the Royal Court has been striving to get the English rights of *Man is Man*. WHY? What is it that bemuses otherwise discerning producers into thinking that everything in the vast, uneven output of Bertolt Brecht, the East German playwright, deserves restaging? The cult is ludicrous! On the evidence of last night, this broad satire on the British Army in India would hardly rate a sketch in a Gang Show... I was not moved emotionally except possibly when Georgia Brown, as a updated Mother Courage with a mobile canteen, briefly struck a Kurt Weill-like vibrato when singing... I smiled bleakly perhaps twice at the feeble army jokes and my positive reaction was one of mounting exasperation... There were good performances by Bob Hoskins, Derek Newark and Trevor Peacock—and an appalling one from Roddy Maude-Roxby (as a panto-style Chin-Chin-Chinaman). And that's about it. Brecht go Home!

CHAPTER 7
'I don't mind type-casting'

Having made minor television history in 1963 by appearing in the first ever episode of *Doctor Who*—as a caveman—with William Hartnell in the original role of the time-travelling doctor, Derek returned to the popular long-running sci-fi series in 1970 on a ten-episode contract playing the character Greg Sutton, opposite Jon Pertwee as the third Doctor Who. Off-camera they made each other laugh a lot and they became good friends. Derek's workload that year included several episodes in *Department S*, a fictitious branch of Interpol that investigated bizarre and supposedly unsolvable crimes. It starred the gay actor Peter Wyngarde as the flamboyantly camp and dandified character Jason King. Derek and Peter did not become friends.

In a one-off drama called *Big Brother*, a London Weekend TV production, Derek played a stern-faced prison officer. He also appeared in two films: *Dad's Army* (a big screen spin-off of the highly successful TV comedy), in which he was perfectly cast as the ramrod, bellowing Regimental Sergeant Major; and *Fragment of Fear*, a thriller starring David Hemmings, Gayle Hunnicut, Flora Robson, and Wilfred Hyde White, supported by Derek Newark, Daniel Massey, and the Italian heavyweight actor Adolfo Celi. In November 1970, he was interviewed by *The Sun* newspaper:

> Derek Newark, guest star in tonight's *Dixon of Dock Green* episode, admits to being typecast. Unlike other actors I've met, he's delighted about it. Derek has a soft spot for the tough, inarticulate types he so often plays. He was the CSM in *Oh! What a Lovely War*, and will plays a wrestler in a play called *The Wedding Gift*, due soon on ITV. Tonight in the episode *The Fighter* he is a boxer, Eddie Brown, heading downhill at the ripe old age of 35 [Derek was 38 at the time].
>
> 'I suppose you could call those last two roles CSMs without uniforms,' he said. 'I don't mind this type-casting because I've proved often enough that I can play other parts.' He will be Detective-Inspector Bryant in Adam Faith's next *Budgie* series, and Willis Hall who wrote the series, has another role for Derek as a football manager in a play for the *Thirty Minute Theatre*. 'His team have just lost 5-0 at home,' said Derek, 'and they're due to play Leeds next. It's a marvellous part.'

The beefy part was that of Wilf Hardiman in the BBC2 production of *They Don't All Open Men's Boutiques* shown in January 1972. Wilf manages a losing football team, but his faith is boundless in his hapless squad at the bottom of Division Four. The play was directed by TV veteran Herbert Wise. Stanley Reynolds reviewed the show for *The Times*:

The entire action took place in the dressing room with the muddied, gormless team being lashed in monologue by the manager, played by Derek Newark, who calls upon them to set their minds in beating Leeds United. It was marvellously funny. How much one wanted to see more of this Fourth Division side. Derek Newark's *tour de force* monologue of illogic was exactly the sort of conversation you can hear any Sunday in season in a northern pub. He stood before his players calling on them like a raving Napoleon or, calming down, he attempted to convince them with his ale house logic.

Holding out his fingers in the true manner of the public house logician he says: 'There are three things we can do. We can lose, we can draw, or we can win.' He counts them off on his fingers. 'So,' he announces proudly, a terrific light of hope dawning on his face, 'no matter how you look at it we're two-to-one on.' Mind was succeeding over matter, personality championing over probability. It's what keeps the supporters of the perpetual losers going.

When he seemed to have won his troops over, there was a rare comic shot with Newark turning his back on the players while on his face was traced a parody of that smile Marlon Brando used in *Julius Caesar* when Mark Antony swayed the mob. Of course, once the manager has left the players sink back into defeat. But there was no pathos in the play, this was full-blooded joyous humour.

In order for Derek to absorb the full atmosphere of the 'beautiful game', albeit at the amateur end, Willis Hall invited Derek to watch a match played by St Albans, of which Hall was president. After the game, Derek spent some time in the dressing room. 'Just listening and watching the guys,' he said, 'gave me stacks of material... I'm not what you'd call an avid football fan.' That visit to St Albans paid off. 'Wilf Hardiman is a man of vision,' wrote reviewer Terry Metcalf, 'a man with the roar of the crowd in his ears... Derek Newark was very good as the tenacious manager and in spite of knowing nothing much about football, I found myself enjoying it thoroughly.'

The play proved popular with the viewing public. Mrs Pat Baldwin of Stockport, Cheshire, was impressed enough to write to Derek care of the BBC in London:

> Dear Mr Newark,
> I am writing to congratulate you on your fine performance in last evening's BBC2 play. It was excellent and my husband and I applaud you and your supporting cast for a splendid thirty minutes entertainment—also thanks to the writer for a first class script. Not being a television addict, I seldom criticise but we so enjoyed your portrayal of the character I felt the least I could do was to write and thank you for all the effort and time you must have spent. With sincere good wishes for your future career.

To keep himself match-fit for the many energetic roles he was called to play, Derek maintained his skill at fencing, both rapier and sabre, with constant practice. He was a regular member of the London Judokwai gymnasium run by Doug Robinson. Judo and karate expert, stuntman and fight arranger, Doug had instructed actress Honor Blackman in her judo moves for *The Avengers* series. Derek worked with Doug in numerous TV action thrillers. Doug's elder brother Joe 'Tiger' Robinson was also an actor/stuntman and former heavyweight wrestling champion. He made his film debut in *A Kid for Two Farthings* (1955), in which he wrestled the gigantic Italian Primo Camera, one-time world heavy weight boxing champion. Joe retained his fighting fitness into advanced age. In 1998, he hit the headlines after fighting off a gang of eight muggers single-handedly. Aged 70, he was alighting from a bus in Cape Town when the gang struck with baseball bats and knives. The 'Tiger' disabled two with flying kicks, karate-chopped another, and broke the arm of a fourth attacker—the rest fled to safety.

January 1972 saw the London premiere of the film *The Offence* at the Odeon Leicester Square, a police drama starring Sean Connery, directed by the American Sidney Lumet from a screenplay by John Hopkins. Derek played Detective Frank Jessard opposite Detective Sergeant Johnson (Connery). It told a gritty story of the brutal, world-weary Johnson and his psychological endeavours to nail a suspected child molester, played by Ian Bannen. The cast included Trevor Howard, Vivien Merchant, Peter Bowles, and John Hallam.

From serious detective to comical cop, in May 1972 Derek reappeared as Detective Inspector Bryant in the new TV series of *Budgie* starring Adam Faith, a mixture of comedy and drama. The first series ended with Bryant putting Budgie in jail. Adam Faith as Ronald 'Budgie' Bird, is a petty criminal, a cheeky Cockney always ducking and diving and dealing in scams that usually fail. The ludicrous Bryant is ever in pursuit of the likeable rogue. To create a comedic appearance, Derek wore his hair slicked back, adopted glasses, and bulky padding to give a chubby look. It was quite a transformation from his usual hard man persona.

Stewart Knowles, star columnist of the *TV Times*, visited Derek at his home in Purley, Surrey, to interview him and found his subject pounding away at a punch-bag hanging in his garage, a distinctively different figure to the plump, maladroit middle-aged Bryant of *Budgie*:

> His fists giving the punch-bag a thrashing, he looked like a man who would anger quickly. His face is an armoury of expressions, many of them aggressive, and it comes as no surprise to learn that he was once a Lance Corporal drill instructor in the Coldstream Guards... He spent most of his five years in the regular army as an officer, having transferred from the Guards to the Royal Army Service Corps, reaching the rank of Acting Captain by the time he ended his service in 1958 and started to train as an actor at RADA and joined the Parachute Regiment as a Territorial.
>
> All through the interview I had that feeling he was going to tell me to get a haircut and march me to the guardroom so fast my feet wouldn't touch the ground! His hair was very short, since he had been playing a

few days earlier the part of a sergeant in the Lancers in the year 1907. A rifle marksman, Newark boxed and played rugby for the army, where he learned to fence. He rides regularly, runs if he thinks he's been smoking too much, plays squash with *Budgie* star Adam Faith.

'To be an actor,' he said, 'you must have the physical potential of an athlete and the constitution of a horse.' He had reached the yellow-belt stage of judo but had to give it up a year ago when he damaged his back diving through a window in Brecht's *Man is Man* at London's Royal Court Theatre. In films, on television and the stage he has played about 160 parts in the 11 years since leaving RADA—nobody does his fighting or stunt work for him. In an episode of *The Persuaders* he took on Roger Moore and had plenty of breath left for Tony Curtis! Last year in a TV film called *Venom*, he played a German 'heavy' dressed in black leather. He had three fights, fell down a flight of stairs...

In a *Dixon of Dock Green* episode recently he played a boxer and insisted on the fight scene being done properly. In the end it ran three times longer than the director had intended... Newark resents any suggestion of being stuck with a very similar range of uniformed parts and when I asked him to name a part as far removed from these as possible, he said: 'Two years ago, at Colchester, I played the Paul Scofield part in *The Staircase*—a raving, 40-year-old "queen" and that is about as far as you can get from a Company Sergeant Major.'

*****

In October 1972, Derek was back in the theatre as the scheming Iago in *Othello* at the Queens Theatre, Hornchurch. The Moor was played by that fine, versatile Welshman Philip Madoc. After studying languages at the University of Wales, Madoc went on to the University of Vienna, where he won the Diploma of the Interpreters Institute. He could speak seven languages, including German, Italian, Russian and Swedish. On deciding a change of career, he enrolled at RADA and was there at the same time as Derek. Madoc made an impressive Othello, his sonorous voice both noble and dramatic. Derek's deceitful Iago was adequate but, at the time, it was my opinion that he spoke his lines too quickly. However, Iago is a demanding role for any actor, being the longest part in all of Shakespeare's plays. Both adaptable actors, Derek and Philip were destined to work together in a number of TV projects over the coming years.

Although Philip Madoc went on to play many leading parts, including the title role in the BBC TV mini-series *The Life and Times of David Lloyd George*, he will, perhaps, be best remembered by the public at large as the menacing German U-boat commander in a celebrated 1973 episode of the comedy series *Dad's Army*. Madoc, having been captured by Captain Mainwaring's Home Guard unit, is taking notes on his treatment as a prisoner-of-war. When Pike, the youngest member of the unit, makes a rude remark about Hitler, Madoc turns on him and demands: 'Your name vill go on the list. Vot is it?' And Mainwaring snaps: 'Don't tell him, Pike!' Madoc died of cancer in his sleep in 2012, aged 77.

In June 1973, Derek found himself in New Scotland Yard—not the famous police headquarters—but a new TV series starring John Woodvine as Detective Chief Superintendent John Kingdom. Derek played the leading guest role as 'Mad Harry' Logan in the episode called *Where's Harry?* Logan, a vicious gangland killer escapes from jail, and top cop Kingdom wants to know who organised his mysterious escape—and why? Such is the merry-go-round of TV casting that in February 1974 Derek re-invented himself from criminal to crime-buster in a leading role as Detective Inspector Tucker, ambitious assistant to his boss, Detective Chief Superintendent Barlow, played by that veteran TV copper, Stratford Johns, who had earned his 'handcuffs' in long-running police series *Z-Cars*, *Softly Softly*, and *Task Force*. The new BBC series was called *Barlow*. The following piece appeared in the 4 March edition of the *South Wales Echo*:

> The newcomer, Detective Inspector Tucker, was brought in by the BBC chiefs, I understand, specifically because they thought that Barlow was no longer able to strike sparks with the viewers. Well, personally I think they were right—both in their fear, and in their remedy. Barlow's snap and zest were indeed slowing down and his programmes no longer had the same appeal. But the importation of Tucker—in the form of Derek Newark—is the best thing that has happened for years. Now there's a new crackle and vitality to the *Barlow* series. If Stratford Johns doesn't watch out Mr Newark will

outshine him. Derek Newark himself, though, cannot see that happening.

'After 12 years a thing like that wouldn't happen easily. Stratford Johns is a superb actor and people have a great liking for the way he has built the Barlow character up. But they do want to do another series with the two of us in it—so that the relationship can be developed. Tucker is as Barlow was 10 years ago. He makes the same sort of mistakes and Barlow recognises this. There's a great similarity between them, Tucker is rude, objectionable and self-opinionated. They are bound to get up each other's noses, and we play on that throughout the present series... Later on, Tucker is to reveal that he isn't such a hard nut as he seems to be, all the same, he has given Barlow something to cope with.

The *Barlow* bandwagon rolled on for a year and then was gone, but Derek was constantly on television in a variety of roles. He made several guest appearances in the new TV sitcom *Rising Damp* starring Leonard Rossiter as the obnoxious landlord of a boarding house. Derek played the wrestler called Spooner. 'Derek Newark, commando-turned actor, occasionally gets the urge to play a real softy,' revealed a report in *The Daily Mirror*. 'But producers just do not see the rugged Mr Newark that way. And it's only now and then that a little mirth is allowed to muscle in... In the ring, Spooner is a fearsome animal. But it is a small cat, called Vienna, that finally counts him out. Newark says: "I trip over the cat and break a leg. I finish up in plaster, flat on my back, annoying everyone in the boarding house by playing my radio too loud."'

BANG OUT OF ORDER!

*****

Early in 1975 he was on the road again, touring in a new farce called *Darling Mr London*, written by Anthony Harriot and Bob Grant and starring David Jason, a rising young talent. Bob Grant, a successful comedy actor was also in the cast as a Curate. Harriot was the author of *No Sex Please, We're British*, a farce that ran for 16 years in the West End and was the longest-running comedy in the history of world theatre.

Derek had known Jason's older actor brother Arthur White for a number of years since Arthur had graduated from RADA. They had worked together and formed a close friendship. David had changed his birth name to Jason in 1965. I met both brothers White in the late 1960s when we were all members of the old Green Room Club for actors in Adam Street, off London's Strand, and I was not impressed by little David's apparent lack of charisma. A decade later he became a national star as Del Boy in the long-running TV series *Only Fools and Horses*.

In *Darling Mr London* Jason played a GPO International Telephone Operator blessed with a magnetic and appealing telephone manner who charms his way into the affections of girls around the world—a Mr Nobody with a catnip voice. Cue a beauty contest with scantily clad girls posing with cod foreign accents. Derek played Jason's supervisor and brother-in-law. The show opened in the industrial town of Billingham, County Durham, some two miles from Stockton-on-Tees. Why Billingham? It was well known in the business as a start-up place for shows hopefully destined for the West End. It was a cheap place for a production on a small and tight budget. The theatre complex included a concert hall, lecture hall, gymnasium and roller-skating rink. With no money for posh hotels, the cast were housed in a nearby tower block originally built to accommodate university students, with spartan rooms each containing a single, narrow, rickety bed. Not, one would have thought, a romantic setting for seduction. But that did not stop Derek from his usual sexual shenanigans.

When on tour, Derek—a married man with two sons—adopted the persona and sexual promiscuity of a bachelor. When touring the country he was never the faithful husband. He was handsome, funny, and virile and there were plenty of pretty girls available in show business. His long-suffering wife Jean chose to ignore this constant weakness of Derek for over twenty years until his womanising became too flagrant to forgive and she finally divorced him.

During the short run of *Darling Mr London*, Derek's roving, randy eye settled on a blonde and beautiful member of the cast, 24-year-old Leena Skoog, Swedish fashion model and singer. She responded willingly to his advances. Jason himself tells the story in his autobiography *David Jason, My Life* (published by Century, 2013). When he knocked on Derek's door to call him to breakfast, his knock was answered by hysterical laughter from within. When Derek opened the door in the nude, Jason espied Leena still lying in bed under the sheets but the bedstead 'was now sloping downwards at a jaunty angle.' Both legs at the foot of the rickety bed had collapsed under the vigorous and lengthy copulation of the couple. Sad to say, that after a brief film career, Leena returned home to Sweden and died of cancer aged only 47 in July 1998.

Derek signed his first contract as a National Theatre player in October 1975 when the NT Company was still housed in the Old Vic Theatre. He would remain a loyal and valued ensemble actor at the NT for the next ten years—a decade of personal dramatic success and drinking devilry. The new purpose-built NT building was designed by Sir Denys Lasdun and erected on London's South Bank. Its Brutalist bunker-like exterior did not meet with universal approval. Prince Charles described the ugly concrete complex as 'a way of building a nuclear power station in the middle of London without anyone objecting.'

The NT building contains three separate theatres. The largest, the Olivier, was designed to have an open stage and a fan-shaped auditorium seating 1,160 people. It was named in honour of Lord Olivier, one of the greatest actors of his time, and the NT's Director during the years before the company's move from the Old Vic to the South Bank. The 890-seat Lyttelton was designed to be more conventional in appearance but with an adjustable proscenium stage. It was named after Oliver Lyttelton, Lord Chandos, first chairman of the National Theatre Board. The smallest auditorium was, in Derek's decade, called the Cottesloe Theatre and held up to 400 people in a simple rectangular room with two tiers of galleries on three sides and a floor space that could be rearranged for actors and audience. It was named after Lord Cottesloe, first chairman of the South Bank Board, responsible to the government for building the National Theatre. In 2014, the Cottesloe was refurbished and renamed the Dorfman Theatre.

Olivier resigned as Director of the NT in 1973 to be succeeded by Peter Hall, founder and former Director of the Royal Shakespeare Theatre. When Bill Bryden was invited by

Hall to direct the initial company of the newly formed Cottesloe Theatre, he reached out to his former troupe of players at the Royal Court and they duly followed him to their new abode. Derek Newark was in the vanguard. He was privileged to be part of the small group of Cottesloe players that performed at the Olivier Theatre at the official opening of the yet uncompleted National Theatre complex.

CHAPTER 8
A National Disaster

The grand opening of the National Theatre took place on the evening of 25 October 1976 in the presence of HM The Queen. The play chosen for this auspicious occasion was an obscure comedy of manners written by the Venetian Carlo Goldoni in 1756 called *Il Campiello* (The Little Square), translated by Susanna Graham-Jones and Bill Bryden. Bill also directed the piece with the aid of his notable assistant-director Sebastian Graham-Jones. The cast included Derek as Fabrizio, a Neapolitan, Gasparina's uncle and guardian. Morag Hood was Gasparina, a young woman who speaks in an affected manner. Beryl Reid played a Widow, as did Peggy Mount. Michael Gough played the Count, and Stephen Rea a Pedlar. Despite this talented cast, the play proved a bad choice for this very special event.

The royal show opened with a discordant blast of Household Cavalry trumpeters. Then the great Laurence Olivier himself strode on stage in the theatre named after him to deliver a long, histrionic and overblown speech of welcome. He left the stage to a standing ovation, backing away from the spotlight so that it illuminated only his expressive, outstretched hands, signifying the passing over of this truly national theatre to the public.

'Larry's fucked-up the show!' Sebastian Graham-Jones remarked to Bryden. 'He's poisoned the audience against the play. Now they don't want to see our actors—they just want more of Olivier!'

With hindsight it was generally acknowledged that the Goldoni piece was a wrong choice for the grand opening. Bryden defended his troupe but admitted that it would have been far better to have fielded a celebrated team of heavyweights such as John Gielgud, Ralph Richardson, Paul Scofield, and Diana Rigg reading poetry and Shakespeare in a short satisfying performance... then off to celebrate with the Queen and Prince Philip.

The critics castigated *Il Campiello*. Sheridan Morley headed his review in *Punch* with 'A NATIONAL DISGRACE... A right old shambles from start to finish. Mr Bryden's determination to play Goldoni's class-conscious jokes in assorted Glaswegian and other accents did not translate well.' Another critic called the play 'A NATIONAL DISASTER!' The formidable Jack Tinker of the *Daily Mail* reported that 'This production is a joyless mess... Goldoni may have said: "My style will always be the same, without elegance or pretension... animated by zeal for my art and inspired by love of the truth." Neither of which requirements Bill Bryden fulfilled with his lamentably under-achieving cast... none of which can squeeze blood out of an evening which remains stubbornly stony.'

The Sunday Times made cruel fun of the play, 'All that glisters is not Goldoni.' Another critic called it 'An empty dish to set before a Queen.' Kenneth Tynan, former literary manager of the NT, found the choice of play 'Perverse to the point of madness.' He crudely described the water flowing from the fountain on stage throughout the action as similar to 'quietly pissing on everything we expected of a National Theatre.'

RB Marriat of *The Stage* reviewed the play with a less jaundiced eye: '*Il Campiello* is a delightful period piece set in a bustling Venetian square in the 18th century. Notable are Peggy Mount and Beryl Reid as the Widows... Michael Gough has the best of it with his bizarre Count... Trevor Ray is Sansuga, a nicely doughty Innkeeper, and Derek Newark, as Gasparina's guardian, protects and condemns with spirited effect.'

Keith Dewhurst, the playwright, attended the premier and recalled the event in his co-authored book (with Jack Shepherd) *Impossible Plays* published in 2006: 'The first person I met in the foyer was Derek Newark, the most valiant of all our actors, who was dressed like a figure from the Commedia [dell Arte] with a live monkey on his wrist. He was hurt and puzzled by the show's [abject] reception—and even the monkey seemed downcast.'

It is said that this royal disappointment left Peter Hall deeply ashamed. The play ran for 27 performances. Bill Bryden admitted the mistake of choice but stoutly defended his players and praised their efforts. Derek agreed with him. 'I'm sure the punters—and the Queen—found it difficult to sit through a long evening of Venetian costumes and wigs poncing around spouting inexplicable dialogue. Yes, it was bad judgement to put on such an esoteric piece, but Bill was pleased with us and that, as far as I'm concerned, is all that matters.'

*****

The NT's Green Room bar opened that year and it came to serve as both fulcrum and forum for the Cottesloe Players who became notorious for their drinking and rumbustious behaviour.

Known collectively as the 'Cottesloe Gang' or 'the Rugby Team' or as 'Bryden's Beasts', the regular cast included actors Jack Shepherd, Mark McManus, Brian Glover, Trevor Ray, Tony Haygarth, Karl Johnson, Gawn Grainger, Kenneth Cranham, Brian Cox, Bob Hoskins, Robert Stephens, Jim Carter and Jimmy Devlin; Bill Bryden and his assistant-director Sebastian Graham-Jones, the playwright Keith Dewhurst and, occasionally the provocative Harold Pinter. Most of them went on to great popularity and stardom in TV and films.

Derek was prominent among this bibulous bunch of competing egos: his brawny, boozy, malevolent presence often dominated the rowdy bar. He was in his element in the company of his Cottesloe peers. They were clever, witty, and bitchy. They all followed football, rugby, and boxing. After the trials and tribulations of rehearsals and performances, Bryden's mob would relax and let off steam in the bar. Bryden would flatter and encourage his troupe (he hardly ever criticised a performance or reproved their unruly behaviour) and would expound and invite suggestions for future experimental plays or productions.

Derek in particular was irrepressible and unconstrained in this convivial milieu. Why should he guard his tongue or his opinions? He was with his workmates... they all loved his company, or so he believed. To those who understood and tolerated his peculiar ways he was indeed an amusing chap. He had a fund of jokes and anecdotes that he delivered in various dialects and accents with experienced comic timing. He could keep you laughing. But he had his dark side. In his cups he often—all too often—turned into a cruel and relentless bully, not knowing or caring when to stop his insults and slurs. One explosive evening in the Green Room he overstepped the imaginary mark. He was bang out of order—and he got his well-deserved comeuppance.

It happened after a gruelling performance of *The Mysteries*, when the actor Sylvester McCoy, who had come to see the play, decided to join the 'Rugby Team' at the Green Room bar. For some reason, Derek had taken an instant dislike to McCoy (destined for stardom as Doctor Who 1987-89) and decided to give the little actor a rough time via the verbals. So virulent was he with his insults that Jim Carter, then in the cast of *The Mysteries* (and later to become internationally famous as Carson the impeccable butler in *Downton Abbey*), could stand the one-sided bullying no longer.

He knocked the utterly surprised Derek to the floor, keeping him pressed down, and threatened to punch his face in if he didn't stop his vicious rant. Carter was bigger, stronger, and fitter than Derek, who was 52 and Carter 15 years younger. Derek was shocked into silence and inaction. He got to his feet and walked out of the hushed bar without a word. Had he been in his physical prime, I have little doubt that the incident would have developed into a blood bath, but Derek was unfit and suffering from chronic knee pain. He did the right thing in swallowing his macho pride and to walk away. Some years later he had a similar confrontation with hard man actor Ray Winstone.

BANG OUT OF ORDER!

The rowdy antics of the Cottesloe 'Rugby Team' often dominated the Green Room bar. Daniel Rosenthal records in his book *The National Theatre Story* (published in 2013):

> Other actors, backstage and staff would sometimes walk into the Green Room, see the Cottesloe stalwarts in full cry, mutter, 'The Rugby Team's in again!' and seek more peaceful surroundings. Stage manager Rosemary Beattie... remembers Cottesloe actors in the bar, 'plastered and giving everybody grief'. Individually [they were] all terribly likeable, but together really badly behaved schoolboys. And Bill [Bryden] didn't exactly set the greatest example.

Bryden always stoutly defended his troublesome troupe of topers by claiming that the NT's other two theatres were riven by jealousy, that his productions were often more successful than those of the Olivier and the Lyttelton. He would protest that the Cottesloe was an easy target for resentment and criticism: 'They all bang on about these hairy-arsed actors in the Green Room, talking too loudly...Yes, we were quite arrogant, but we never stopped working very hard. People probably hated us. Peter Hall never did.' It has been said that Hall had a relish for talented hooligans and treated them with a 'sort of benevolent diffidence'.

Throughout his ten years at the National, Derek established a reputation for his hard drinking and out-of-order capers. When Simon Callow was cast as Mozart in the Peter Shaffer play *Amadeus* at the National, he was greeted by the Cottesloe

BANG OUT OF ORDER!

Derek John Newark, aged five.

Derek at 15, the tallest of the Romford school team (top row, third from left).

At 16, Derek joined the Merchant Navy.

BANG OUT OF ORDER!

A born entertainer! Derek at 18 posing in Paris, 1951.

BANG OUT OF ORDER!

Lance-Corporal Newark,
Coldstream Guards, June 1954.

Regimental Sergeant Major
Ronald Brittain, Coldstream
Guards, the 'Loudest Voice
in the Army'.

2nd Lieutenant DJ Newark,
Royal Army Service Corps,
March 1955.

BANG OUT OF ORDER!

Derek's stand-up comedy alter ego: 'Laughs and Smiles with Jackie Styles'. Singapore show business 1956.

JACKIE STYLES.
Well known in London as a Night-Club Entertainer.

ROYAL ACADEMY OF DRAMATIC ART
Summer Season, 1960

LITTLE THEATRE, Central Avenue, BANGOR.
Presented by CEMA and BANGOR BOROUGH COUNCIL.

Derek, centre, in *Rookery Nook*, a farce by Ben Travers.

The Three Musketeers: Derek as Porthos, Daniel Massey (centre) as Athos, and Richard Hampton as Aramis. Nottingham Playhouse, November 1962.

BANG OUT OF ORDER!

Derek threatens to shoot an officer as the mixed-up Private Varley in the TV production of *End of Conflict*.

BANG OUT OF ORDER!

Playing Joe Harwood, newspaper reporter, in *Front Page Story* TV series of 1965.

Derek in his first German officer role, as Ziegel in the Twentieth-Century Fox film, *The Blue Max*, of 1966.

Newark—working out in a judo club

Seen working out at the London Judokwai gymnasium is Derek Newark who appears this week as a prison warder in *Big Brother*. In our picture he is seen in the arms of gymnasium owner and judo expert Douglas Robinson. Newark forever plays hoods. "Presumably," he says, "because that's how I look."

Before becoming an actor he was five years a regular soldier and now makes a point of keeping fit. Riding, fencing, judo. "As an actor I have to keep fit. I'm so often called on to do such outrageous things."

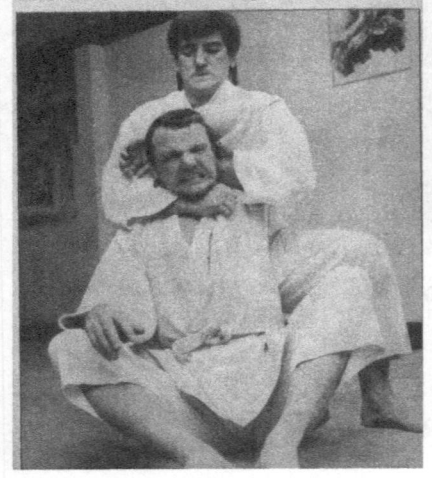

Derek and Dougie Robinson featured in *TV Times*, September 1970.

BANG OUT OF ORDER!

Padded-out to play the pudgy policeman Inspector Bryant, always chasing cheeky rascal Adam Faith in the TV comedy series *Budgie*, 1971-72.

Derek played Detective Constable Jessard, assistant to Detective Sergeant Johnson (Sean Connery) in *The Offence*, directed by Sidney Lumet, a Tantallion Film released by United Artists in 1972.

Playing Groucho Marx in *The Groucho Letters*, a Platform Performance at the National Theatre from November 1977 to January 1978.

The author with Derek at *Sardi's* famous show business restaurant after the opening night of *Bedroom Farce* on Broadway, March 1979.

Poster for *Bedroom Farce* at London's Prince of Wales Theatre in 1978, prior to its North American tour.

A swashbuckling Derek as Robolledo, a soldier in *The Mayor of Zalamea*, at the Cottesloe Theatre in August 1981.

In the exacting role of Martin Bormann, Nazi leader, with Maurice Roeves who played Hess, in the TV drama *Inside the Third Reich*, 1982.

Is this really Derek Newark? As the ugly sister Gloria (right) in the National Theatre pantomime *Cinderella*, in December 1983. With Robert Stephens as ugly sister Euphoria.

Derek on the programme cover of *Glengarry Glen Ross* in which he gave his best ever stage performance as the salesman Shelley Levene. It ran from September 1983 to May 1986.

GOLDEN BOY JEREMY FLYNN *as Joe Bonaparte* DEREK NEWARK *as Tom Moody*

Cartoon by Hewison published in *Punch* magazine of May 1984.

Bellman and True paperback novel by Desmond Lowden (Thames Methuen). Cover shows Derek Newark assaulting leading man Bernard Hill in the film of the book, 1987.

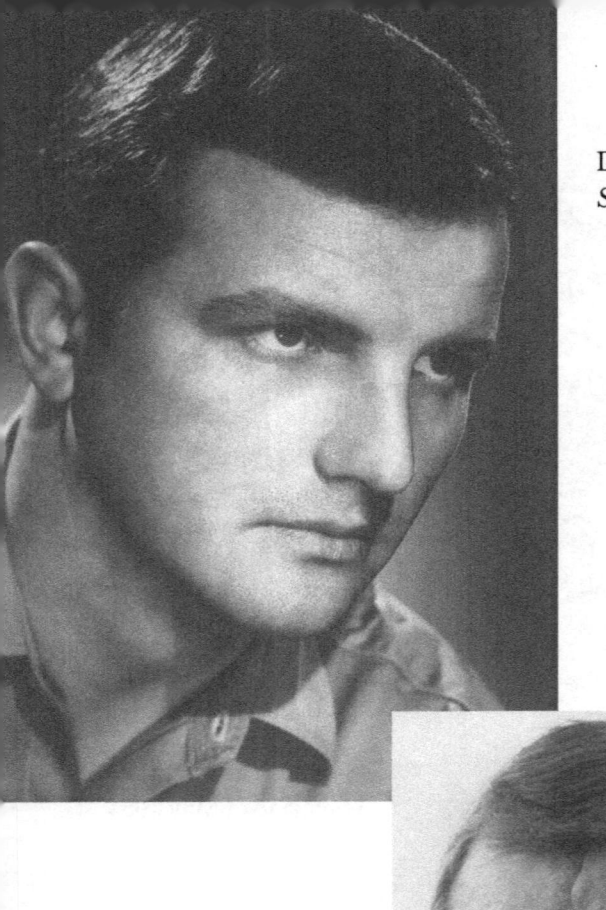

Derek's handsome *Spotlight* photograph, 1965.

The unforgettable face of a veteran thespian, 1995.

actor James Grant, as Callow recalled in his memoirs, *My Life in Pieces*, published in 2010:

> 'Hi, Simon,' he said, 'Welcome to the Green Room. See that hole over there, in the carpet? That's where Derek Newark falls.' This was an allusion to the tall, notoriously bibulous actor who was one of the key members of Bill Bryden's company at the Cottesloe... to which both James Grant and the so frequently horizontal Derek Newark belonged.

In their funny and revealing book *Impossible Plays*, co-authors Keith Dewhurst and Jack Shepherd record the performances and the eccentricities of the Cottesloe years. Dewhurst related how the Green Room 'Rugby Team' players, plus directors, stage staff, and other actors including the female gender, attended a regular meeting of what was crudely dubbed 'The Cunt of the Month Club', held at lunchtime in the NT boardroom. The award was a piece of amethyst quartz on a chain. The winner of this un-coveted prize was, in Dewhurst's words, 'the person deemed to have broken the Green Room social code in the most obnoxious fashion'. Mark McManus wore the chain of shame on one occasion for, it is said, relieving his bladder outside Buckingham Palace. It comes as no surprise to learn that Derek won the award twice for being wantonly out of order... 'and was given the trophy outright, which brought the club to an end.'

*****

BANG OUT OF ORDER!

Apart from its main productions, the NT in Derek's time, encouraged short 'Platform' performances: one-man essays, talks, poetry readings, and such in the early evenings in each of the three theatres. Derek was among the first platform volunteers. He decided that a light dose of self-criticism of the NT would be the order of the day. An internal notice informed the house: 'Derek Newark (the Green Room's answer to Max Hastings) will be working on *The Enemy Within*. Tuesday November 2nd. Rehearsal Room 3 at 6.00pm for 30 minutes. All are Welcome.'

The *London Evening News* ran this item on 12 November 1976:

Who says that the National Theatre is too solemn and pompous? Full marks to the top brass for allowing actor Derek Newark to send up his boss, Peter Hall and the concrete edifice next month. Mr Newark, a straight actor who plays Inspector Tucker in *Barlow* on TV and is in *Il Campiello* and *Tamburlaine* for the National has a sideline as a stand-up comic. Backstage he can paralyse a 'pro' audience with his throwaway wit. So he has been invited to give special pre-show performances for the public at the Lyttelton Theatre on December 7, 10, and 29. His 'I say' comedy will last for one hour, starting at 6pm and costing 30p a ticket. Newark calls it *The Enemy Within* and he says his targets (treated affectionately—he wants to work again!) will be Peter Hall and the National.

Derek's Platform Performance embraced humorous anecdotes and barbed criticisms on his life in the Army, the Merchant Navy, the theatre in general and Peter Hall and the NT in particular. James Green of the *Evening News* had this to say:

> Here's a novelty—Hamlet wanting to play the clown. Derek Newark is a National Theatre straight actor who has a backstage reputation as a patter comedian. Sample: To effect economy the National will be presenting *One Gentleman of Verona*, and *All's Well That Ends Quickly*. Most of his arrows are reserved for National chief Peter Hall, who has responded by inviting him to present a pre-show 6pm cabaret spot... Mr Newark calls the National 'Hall's Folly' and says that Hall, known as 'Jaws' walks across the water from the cultural ghetto to his home at the Barbican. Mr Newark's 'That's life' gentle humour is engagingly delivered, but he will need more present-day material if he is eventually to lead a National Theatre cabaret team.

The Times Diary reported that:

> The criticism was gentle and good-humoured and occupied only the last 10 minutes of the hour-long solo. It was in fact the least effective bit of the performance. The first 50 minutes was made up of skilful anecdotes about Newark's theatrical past, which the audience enjoyed. But he changed his style for the in-house stuff, doing it as a series of one-line gags. The jokes—largely

to do with Peter Hall's alleged delusions of grandeur—were too old, and told too self-consciously, to really strike home. They lacked venom and conviction. And afterwards, Newark and Hall chatted cosily at the bar like the friends they clearly are. Still, Newark's performance is worth seeing.

From the very start, Derek was a hard-working, conscientious member of the Cottesloe Company, putting in long hours at the NT building and taking little time off for family life or holidays. But it was not onerous labour for he thrived in the theatrical environment. He liked his fellow team players. He admired and respected Bill Bryden. He enjoyed drinking with his mates in the Green Room. A key member of the Cottesloe team, he still wanted to be the best of the bunch. He spent so much time at the National that it became, virtually, his second home. In between rehearsals and his first Platform Performance, he received the following letter dated 8 November 1976:

Dear Derek,
I know you think we're very quaint the way we behave over holidays and holiday money, but I thought, just for the record, I ought to write and confirm what is happening next week. It is, as you know, a holiday week for you. And, as chance would have it, it is also the week in which we will be paying you three weeks' holiday money because of not having been able to give you a holiday for a year. The actual holiday week

doesn't affect your money at all— normal basic salary is paid as usual—but we shall be including that money for the previous year with your salary on Thursday, 18th November. I will send your agent a copy of this letter so that she too knows what is happening. With best wishes, Jean Anscombe Assistant to Michael Hallifax [Head of Company & Planning]

Michael Kustow, Associate Director of Projects and instigator of the Platform Performances, encouraged Derek to take part in them. Much to Derek's delight, Kustow suggested an evening of Kipling's *Barrack Room Ballads*. In September 1977, he in company with Warren Clarke and Kenneth Cranham dressed as Victorian red-coated 'Tommy Atkins', read the verses, some of which had been lightly orchestrated by Richard Mangan between single voices and various combinations. Derek did a solo *Gunga Din* and the trio sang the musical version of *The Road to Mandalay*. 'They could hardly have done it better,' said *The Financial Times*. 'They certainly pleased the audience, who broke into hearty song when asked to join in the chorus of *Mandalay*. It was heartening, I thought, to find such sympathy for the troops in this overwhelmingly anti-fighting age.'

The famous Groucho Marx died in August 1977 aged 86. He was the cigar chomping, wisecracking member of the Marx Brothers comedy team who made film audiences laugh in a series of madcap movies in the 1930s and 1940s. Groucho had a long career in show business and mastered every entertainment medium from vaudeville to radio to television. The voluble comedian was also a prolific and witty writer of letters to a legion of prominent people. Shortly after his death, Michael Kustow, an ardent admirer of Groucho, decided to write and produce a Platform tribute to his comic hero, a one-man show based on his coruscating correspondence. And who better to speak the words of the celebrated humourist than Derek Newark. It proved an excellent choice.

Derek tackled the Groucho challenge with his usual thoroughness. He studied the Marx Brothers movies and read all the relevant books. Groucho was born and named Julius in October 1890. He had five brothers, one died as a child. Their father was Samuel Marx, a humble Jewish tailor of little or no ambition, and the family lived in poverty in a flat on East 93rd Street, New York. Julius early developed a grouchy, moody nature and thus gained his nickname. From early vaudeville touring days the Marx Brothers progressed to make a series of successful movies.

Always the cynic, always the pessimist, Groucho once met a priest who said 'I want to shake your hand and thank you for all the pleasure you've brought into the world.' Groucho responded with 'And I want to shake your hand and thank you for all the pleasure you've taken out of the world.' On another occasion he told a journalist, 'I wouldn't live my life over again for a million dollars... unless, of course, it were tax free.'

Groucho was a challenging role for any actor. Derek himself was surprised when selected for the part. On 2 December 1977, Glenys Roberts, show-business writer on the *London Evening News* reported that:

BANG OUT OF ORDER!

This is how Derek Newark's latest platform performance, *The Groucho Letters*, happened. Director-writer Michael Kutstow immediately realised when he heard of the comedian's death, that in Derek he had a splendid Groucho— with that rarest of talents in an English actor, a perfect American accent.

'If someone had said "You're going to play Groucho",' Newark exclaimed, 'I'd have said "Never!" It was only because Michael knew enough about me and knew I could do it. But I couldn't have done it unless I had been a stand-up comic years ago.'

It was not a major production and the critics gave it mixed reviews. *Punch* magazine praised it as 'Another National treasure that should not be missed: an arrangement by Michael Kustow of *The Groucho Letters* [published in book form in 1967] immaculately performed by Derek Newark as Groucho and Glyn Grain as his long-suffering stooge... it is one of the funniest shows in town.' *The Sunday Times* was much more analytical in its review:

> There is a strange oddment to be seen as a Platform Performance at the National Theatre: *The Groucho Letters*, read by Derek Newark... Mr Newark, despite the greasepaint moustache, frockcoat and cigar, neither looks like Groucho nor sounds like him, nor can he get the famous lope right. Moreover the gags, as opposed to excerpts from Groucho's correspondence, are

disastrous. Yet the 45 minutes are worth it for one thing. This is not the famous correspondence with Warner Brothers, the letters are indeed very funny... But what gives *The Groucho Letters* real theatrical quality is a single, long letter which Groucho wrote in his old age and retirement to a friend who had asked how he passed his days. The fantasy [of his daily boring routine] spills out with all Groucho's wit and style, but gradually we realise that what we are listening to is a cry of despair, and that beneath the jokes is a man in the unbearable pain of loneliness, boredom and the fear that everything is meaningless. Derek Newark reads it beautifully, his voice now an aged croak, and the audience froze as the mask fell away. Ridi, Pagliaccio; *la commedia e finita.*

The Groucho Letters ran at the NT from early November 1977 to the end of January 1978—a total of six performances. Richard Huggett of the Arts Theatre Club in Great Newport Street, London, sent Derek a personal letter dated 31 January 1978:

Dear Derek,
Warmest congratulations on your GROUCHO, and let me say I think it's one of the best things you've done (and I speak as a long term admirer). I do hope that one of the TV companies is going to show a little enterprise and foresight and film it for posterity (shall I suggest it?). I wrote to Elaine Dundy [the writer and first wife of Peter Finch] and suggested that she should make the trip from Australia to see it. She wrote back saying she

was far too busy working on her biography of 'bloody' Peter. Ah well, her loss... [*Finch, Bloody Finch* by Elaine Dundy was published in 1980]

In June 1978, Derek reprised his role in *Plunder*, a farce written by the legendary Ben Travers, a revival of the successful NT production of 1976. The play, originally staged in 1928, is the fourth of a string of Travers' farces that filled the Aldwych Theatre in the 1920s. *Plunder* is a comic period piece about a gentleman crook. Derek played Chief Detective Inspector Sibley in both productions. Others in the cast included Frank Finlay, Dinsdale Landen, Trevor Ray, Dandy Nichols, Diana Quick, Polly Adams, and Brenda Blethyn. Michael Blakemore directed, assisted by Sebastian Graham-Jones. The first lot of tickets to arrive at the box office promised admission to a play called 'Blunder'—the error was spotted just in time for a reprint.

Princess Margaret was guest of honour at the 1976 opening staged at the Lyttelton. The production was a great success. *The Daily Mirror* praised it as 'A glorious piece of precision farce.' Sheridan Morley of *Punch* magazine considered it 'The funniest evening to be found anywhere in London.' The Princess so enjoyed the show that she made a return visit with friends. The combined 1976 and 1978 productions of *Plunder* ran to 127 performances, ending on 20 January 1979. Ben Travers, born in 1886 and still active in the theatre world, wrote a hand-written letter to Derek dated 6 November 1978:

BANG OUT OF ORDER!

Dear Derek,
This is to express my gratitude to you for the great contribution you have made towards the success of *Plunder* both in its first and second innings at the National. The Scotland Yard scene, which is the high-spot of the show, depends to a tremendous extent on your part and it was due to your perfect playing of it that all that sequence of wonderful laughs was brought about! So my best thanks and good wishes for a happy spell with curtains aplenty at the Prince of Wales and in all your future shows.

Praise indeed from a master of light farce. His reference to the Prince of Wales Theatre concerned the new Alan Ayckbourn play, *Bedroom Farce*, in which Derek also appeared. Ben Travers died in 1980 aged 94; his last work, a comedy called *The Bed Before Yesterday* was produced in 1976. Ayckbourn, like Travers, made his name with a string of successful comedic plays including *Relatively Speaking, How the Other Half Loves, Absurd Person Singular*, and the trilogy *The Norman Conquests*.

June 1978 was a very busy month for Derek: rehearsing *Bedroom Farce* morning and afternoon and appearing in *Plunder* in the evenings. *Bedroom* opened on 23 June at the Lyttelton. The *mise en scene* was a single set of three bedrooms, in three different homes, set side-by-side on stage. In the first bedroom are the oldest couple, Ernest (Michael Gough) and Delia (Joan Hickson). In the middle room are Malcolm (Derek Newark) and Kate (Susan Littler). The third bedroom is that of Nick (Michael Stroud) and Jan (Polly Adams) into which blunder a fourth couple, Trevor (Stephen Moore) and Susannah (Delia Lindsay) to create more havoc. The action takes place one long crazy Saturday night. The cast changed a few members during its long run of 185 performances at the NT and its eleven weeks at the Prince of Wales Theatre. But the cast mentioned above was the most constant and most memorable and the one that took the play on its successful American tour of 1979. The play was directed throughout its run, both in the UK and USA, by Ayckbourn and Peter Hall.

Bedroom Farce was an ensemble triumph. All the players were superb. The London critics and the paying public loved the madcap antics. Herbert Kretzmer of the *Daily Express* made the bold statement 'If you don't laugh, sue me.' Milton Shulman of the *Evening Standard* wrote: 'Derek Newark as a beefy extrovert dismayed to discover that while he is sexually performing his wife is only thinking of laying carpets, is a model of conventional male insensitivity.' John Walker of the *International Herald Tribune* said 'All members of the cast performed splendidly; I particularly enjoyed Derek Newark's apoplectic DIY handyman.'

Derek's comic acting impressed the great Harold Pinter, who recalled 'I almost fell out of my seat with laughter when the piece of do-it-yourself furniture that had taken Derek [as Malcolm] ages to construct, collapsed in front of him. The depth of his paralysed, pained disbelief was excruciatingly funny, a masterful demonstration of the essential gravity of farce.'

It was one of Derek's standout roles and would take him on a trip to a stage he'd always dreamed of—Broadway.

CHAPTER 9
A Bedroom on Broadway

After eleven packed weeks at the Prince of Wales in London, *Bedroom Farce* embarked on its grand North American tour, presented by Whitehead-Stevens, George W George, and Frank Milton. The 1979 tour started in Canada in January with a four-week stay at the Royal Alexandra Theatre in Toronto. To celebrate what would be the 300th performance of the play, Peter Hall took his players to the Whalers Wharf restaurant for Sunday dinner before the opening and arranged a suite at the Royal York for dinner after the opening.

Gina Mallet of the *Toronto Star* began her review of 23 January:

> The expression is 'achingly funny'—that's when you can't stop laughing, or someone won't let you. Last night at the Royal Alexandra Theatre, the National Theatre

Company of Great Britain bustled on stage with Alan Ayckbourn's *Bedroom Farce* and immediately set about creating mayhem. In charge of the riot is an actress named Joan Hickson who has the face of an elegant prune and the voice of a wailing violin... Susan Littler and Derek Newark as a couple torn between saws and sex were almost as irresistible as Gough and Hickson doddering around their bedroom.

It set the tone for a triumphant tour that gathered praise in almost every city. In Washington DC, the play opened at the Elsenhower Theater at the Kennedy Center from 20 February till 24 March and the *Washington Post* mentioned in particular Michael Gough, Joan Hickson, and the delightful Susan Littler: 'Enchanting is the only word for Susan Littler, as the guiless, trusting Kate. Littler has a broad, open face, topped by blonde bangs and a knot at the top of her head. With gruff, blustering Derek Newark as her partner, Littler's trustful little smiles will touch your heart and I for one can't wait to see her again.'

After four sell-out weeks in dignified Washington the play moved to brash and brilliant Broadway, the mecca of show business. It opened on 29 March at the Brooks Atkinson Theatre, so-named after a famous critic of *The New York Times*. Douglas Watt theatre critic of the *New York Daily News* was in the first night audience:

> Alan Ayckbourn's *Bedroom Farce* which spread hilarity through the Atkinson last night is a masterly comic construction, inventive enough to make Feydeau's

cheeks burn in his grave... The all-British cast —which will be gradually replaced by American players after nine weeks—is exemplary... Derek Newark is magnificent in his bursts of rage as he endeavors to assemble a desk as a gift for his tired wife Kate, a delightful ninny of enormous appeal as set forth by Susan Littler.

William B Collins of the *Philadelphia Inquirer* wrote that 'Alan Ayckbourn is an enemy of sleep and a friend of laughter... Susan Littler gives a delicious impression of dawning consciousness as her husband Derek Newark works through the night assembling that fragile desk...' Jack O'Brian, the *Voice of Broadway*, was yet another Littler fan: 'Susan Littler is a fine, funny Ayckbourn central clown. She is a bottomless fund of comic reactions, full of contented disbelief at the conniptions mounting steadily, inexorably.' Alan Wallach of the New York *Newsweek* reported that 'The British cast, expertly directed by Ayckbourn and Peter Hall, is marvellous... It's almost unfair to single out the deftest among them. But mention should be made of Susan Littler's Kate, whose face can become a mask of incomprehension when it suits her, and the choked fury of Derek Newark as Malcolm when confronted with a balky guest or a piece of wood.' Richard Eder of *The New York Times* observed 'Derek Newark's lumbering, explosive and kind Malcolm and the engagingly blank Kate of Susan Little are another most enchanting and very funny couple.'

At that particular golden time, *Bedroom Farce* was the National Theatre's longest-running play after its initial opening at the Lyttelton in March 1977. It had been taken up by 30

English repertory companies during 1979 alone. The deal with the American presenters ensured that the NT cast would be retained for the first 14 weeks of its New York run, then to be gradually replaced with American players by the 20th week. The American cabal would be liable for the costs of production and the fees to players and playwright and the co-directors Ayckbourn and Peter Hall. The NT would receive five per cent of gross box-office takings for the first $75,000 each week and 30 per cent thereafter. The play took $95,000 in its first week in Washington. Broadway tickets were priced at $17.50 week nights and $18.50 weekend nights. It was estimated at the time that *Bedroom Farce*, with a four-year run in both London and New York would earn the NT £250,000.

I had planned to see the first night of the New York show and booked a Manhattan hotel for a week. After all, it was a significant moment in Newark family history—brother Derek performing on Broadway. To celebrate the successful opening, the American presenters invited the cast to a late-night supper at *Delsomma's* restaurant next door to the theatre. Derek took me as his guest. We drank with and talked to many prominent actors who attended the supper, as well as the famous playwright Tennessee Williams, to whom Derek—full of his own importance of the moment—deliberately confused with the popular singer Tennessee Ernie. The famous writer received the 'joke' with wry amusement... and moved on. We met Angela Lansbury who was appearing in the hit musical *Sweeney Todd* at the Uris Theatre. Also Simon Ward (*Young Winston*, 1970) with whom Derek had worked at the NT and on TV. Ward had opened at the Palace Theatre in *A Meeting at the River* by Christopher Isherwood, alongside Sam Jaffe, the 86-year-old Hollywood veteran who had played the eponymous role in the 1939 film *Gunga Din*. Both appeared in the Isherwood play that was panned by the critics and closed down after only a few performances. Such are the capricious vagaries of Broadway.

The 4 April edition of *Variety*, that herald of show business, proclaimed that, 'Not in several years have Broadway first-nighters laughed as hard and consistently as at *Bedroom Farce*, last Thursday night's opening with its original London cast, is the season's first all-out smash hit…The all-British cast is superb, the standouts possibly being Michael Gough and Joan Hickson as the oldest couple, apparently 60-ish. Their expertly timed underplaying is an object lesson in the acting profession…'

As a sidebar to their main performance in *Bedroom*, Michael Gough and Derek performed at the American Place Theatre in its regular Lunchtime Humor Show. Devised by Kingsley Amis and Michael Kustow and directed by the latter, the show was called *Kingsley Amis' Nosegay of Light Verse*, and was originally a Platform Performance at the NT in London. The programme included work by Lord Byron, WH Auden, Lewis Carroll, GK Chesterton, John Betjeman, Noel Coward and TS Eliot. Richard F Shepard of *The New York Times* paid a visit in early April:

> What a splendid and simple idea it is, to take two visiting British actors with marvellous voices and have them do poetry readings at lunchtime at the cozy Subplot Cabaret of the American Place Theater… Michael Gough and Derek Newark sit on chairs on a low stage and read 22 selections by poets ranging from that old

tireless poet, Anonymous, to other almost as ubiquitous wordsmiths... although most of it is humorous, some of it, such as one advising against having children, by Philip Larkin, and another about those who have died, by Mr Amis, will not provoke chuckles. The two readers are a most felicitous couple: Mr Gough, silver-haired in thatch and mustache, dresses informally in sports jacket, loafers and such, and Mr Newark, a more stocky sort, wears suit and tie. Mr Gough has a deep resonant voice and an elegantly relaxed manner and infuses the lines with a delicious sense of irony. Mr Newark is more intense and mugs wonderfully both facially and, if one may apply the term, vocally... Both fling themselves, as a team, into limericks, some off-color, but on the mark, and perform brilliantly with a comic Noel Coward elegy, *There Are Bad Times Just Around the Corner*. It all makes for a delightful and low caloric lunch.

Don Nelsen of the New York *Daily News* regaled his readers with this entertaining piece of reportage:

No program pretending to be light verse could possibly escape a reading of Lewis Carroll's *Jabberwocky* and sure enough it was served up by Newark with an impish delight. Both men got to work on that melodramatic Victorian music-hall tear jerker, *She was Poor but She was Honest*. In a performance that cried out for violin accompaniment, Gough and Newark straight-faced the story of a poor working girl seduced and abandoned by a wicked Lord then reviled by a callous society. The last few lines, spoken with utmost seriousness, tells the story: 'It's the same the whole world over... It's the poor what gets the blame.' A robust Newark intoned the words in appropriate lower-class accent...

Derek had high hopes that he and his stage wife Susan Littler might outshine the other cast members and win Tony Awards for their contribution to the great success of *Bedroom Farce*. But it was not to be. The awards of 1979 went to Michael Gough and Joan Hickson. Sad to relate, the promising career of the winsome Susan Littler who had won the hearts and plaudits of the tough Broadway critics, came to an end in July 1982 when she died of cancer at the young age of 34. The *Daily Telegraph* described her early death as 'the greatest premature loss of a British actress since Kay Kendall'— the vivacious film star, married to Rex Harrison, who died of leukaemia in 1959 aged 33. In October 1982, Albert Finney hosted a special programme to honour Susan Littler's memory at the National Theatre in aide of cancer research.

I can't speak for the rest of the cast of *Bedroom Farce*, but I know that the 45-year-old Derek thoroughly enjoyed his time in New York. To be an essential part of a smash-hit on Broadway was for him a youthful dream come true. Proof positive that he was at the top of his game. Earning $2,000 per week, strolling along Broadway to the Brooks Atkinson Theatre made him feel somewhat like *The Man Who Broke the Bank at Monte Carlo*. To compound his sense of success, he proudly dressed like an archetypical Englishman: blue blazer or dark suit, Guards necktie, and polished leather shoes—all that was missing was a bowler hat and furled umbrella!

Being on tour, far away from family ties and obligations, he lived the temporary life of a virtual bachelor and very quickly acquired two regular girlfriends, one a budding actress and the other a wisecracking nightclub singer. His freewheeling bachelor life, however, was interrupted by the planned arrival of his wife Jean and their two teenage sons in April for a two-week stay. He booked them into the Mayflower Hotel overlooking Central Park and moved in with them. He kept his girlfriends out of the frame and played the role of perfect husband and father. They saw all the sights and sounds of the Big Apple together. They took the Circle Line boat around Manhattan and flew in a helicopter over the skyscrapers. They saw Derek's shows and met lots of celebrities. Jean and the boys returned home with happy memories of a wonderful trip. Derek stayed on at the Mayflower, renting a studio room for $1000 per month for the remainder of the *Bedroom* run.

My week in New York was both enjoyable and profitable. During the day I visited the usual tourist sights and took photographs of famous landmarks and ordinary New Yorkers, policemen, firemen, cab drivers, and building workers. All making excellent stock for my professional collection of photographs to be ultimately reproduced by the publishing industry. By night, with his performance at the theatre over, Derek and I would seek out agreeable piano bars and clubs, many of which did not close until 3.00 or 4.00am. At a club called *Oliver Twist* we were surprised and delighted to find that the resident pianist was Lennie Metcalfe, a jazz musician we had known in our youthful bebop days in the London jazz venues of *Club Eleven* and the *Feldman Club* of some thirty years before.

In those far-off days, tall, skinny Lennie in his America-style clothes and crew cut hair was the embodiment of 'cool'. Now he was middle-aged, mortgaged in Manhattan, banging-out boozy tunes to half-pissed Brits—*Roll Out the Barrel*, *Show Me the Way to Go Home*, *Down at the Old Bull and Bush* and *Nellie Dean*. In between the tourist stuff, he would play jazz classics. A culture clash if ever I've heard one: Thelonious Monk and Dizzy Gillespie to Cockney 'Corblimey!' He was pleased to see us and happy to talk about old friends and London jazzmen. Derek mentioned Leon Roy, Lennie's former close mate and drummer, 'He's now managing a condominium in Florida. I see him now and again when he's in town.' Names came tumbling out: Lennie Bush, the double bassist; Tubby Hayes, tenor sax; Cab Kaye, jazz singer; Ray Ellington, drummer and later comedian; and of course the top sax players of the time, Ronnie Scott and Johnny Dankworth. We stayed at the *Oliver Twist until* the wee small hours of the morning. Derek liked the place a lot and—like Oliver—went back for more.

We found another agreeable piano bar called the *Chateau Bahia*, on First Avenue opposite the United Nations Building. The resident pianist-singer was Richard Shadroui, a smiling, 40-ish gay who immediately had a crush on Derek, the current Broadway celebrity. After Derek put him straight about his heterosexuality, the two became platonic buddies and the place became Derek's favourite watering hole. It was also the scene of Derek's violent farewell to New York City.

BANG OUT OF ORDER!

As far as I'm aware—until this bloody curtain-closing finale—Derek's tour had not given rise to any personal out-of-order incidents. But knowing Newark, I suppose there had to be one. On the eve of departure with the rest of the cast, Derek was drinking alone late at night in Shadroui's bar, sitting next to the piano. He fell into conversation with a sad-looking, English-speaking Iranian from the UN building nearby. According to Derek's version of events, he said to Richard in jocular manner, 'Why not play *In a Persian Market* for my Persian friend... it might cheer him up?' And both Derek and Richard laughed at the banter...

The grim-faced Iranian, however, considered the suggestion to be a grave insult to him and his country and started ranting at them. Derek tried to placate the angry man but to no avail. The manager and a bouncer escorted the aggrieved Persian out of the club, but as he left he threatened to wait for Derek outside to settle the matter with physical force, or words to that effect. Soon after, an agitated Derek said, 'Fuck this Arab—if he wants a fight, he'll have it!' And he marched outside to find the man waiting.

Without further ado, Derek launched his brawny 15-stones at the enemy and a violent fistfight ensued. After a few frantic seconds Derek knocked his opponent to the ground and the combat was over as far as he was concerned, and battered and bloodied he left the scene in a hurry. When I saw him in London a few days later to hear the story, I witnessed his badly bruised knuckles and contused face.

CHAPTER 10
Best Ever Performance

With the American adventure over, it was back to experimental work at the NT, back with his mates at the Cottesloe, back to drinking in the Green Room. A few days before he left the States, he received a telegram from Peter Hall: 'Dear Derek many congratulations on such a successful tour. My thanks to you and look forward to seeing you in your Vietnam fatigues.'

Hall was referring to the new Cottesloe production of the book *Dispatches* about the Vietnam War by American journalist Michael Herr. Derek played the part of General Westmoreland. It was not a standout role for him but the play was considered an experimental success and ran from 6 June to 28 July. The remainder of 1979—14 November to 29 December—was taken up with the production of *Candleford*, based on a book of Victorian rural life by Flora Thompson, adapted by Keith Dewhurst. Derek played several parts in a lukewarm creation that ran for 33 performances.

As an associate director of the National Theatre (1973-83), Harold Pinter was free to direct independent productions. His new play of 1980, *The Hothouse*, was staged at the Hampstead Theatre and Pinter directed his own work. Impressed by Derek's serio-comic ability, Pinter chose him to lead the seven-character cast.

'I wrote *The Hothouse* in the winter of 1958,' Pinter explained. 'I put it aside for further deliberation and made no attempt to have it produced at the time. I then went on to write *The Caretaker*. In 1979, I re-read *The Hothouse* and decided it was worth presenting on the stage. I made a few cuts but no changes.' Derek's contract allowed him to work in TV, films, and other stage productions outside the confines of the NT.

The Hampstead Theatre at London's Swiss Cottage Centre was run by the Hampstead Theatre Ltd, a company that received financial support from the Arts Council of Great Britain and the London Borough of Camden. David Aukin was director of the theatre. *The Hothouse* is set in a mysterious and sinister government asylum for unseen 'patients' known only by their numbers. Derek played the part of the man in charge, the enigmatic Colonel Roote. James Grant (also on leave from the Cottesloe) played Gibbs, Roote's baneful, Iago-like deputy. The play opened on 1 May 1980. It received mixed reviews. Robert Cushman of *The Observer* compared it with *The Caretaker*:

What *The Hothouse* most clearly demonstrates is that

The Caretaker which followed it was a glorious sidetrack. Mr Pinter has never matched its marvellous equipoise of character, language and feeling. And it's worth remembering that no subsequent playwright has come up with anything to match its critical and popular impact. Pinter has remained with us as a glory and an embarrassment: a major talent producing minor plays... He benefits from the presence in the dominant role of Derek Newark, as forthright and un-Pinteresque an actor as you could find, who transmits a glorious bovine bewilderment. Others are more conventionally icy, the honours going to James Grant, *suaviter in modo*, and Angela Pleasance, a stunningly cool devil-woman.

John Barber of *The Daily Telegraph* wrote: 'Obvious but amusing fun is made of the bull-necked colonel capitally presented by Derek Newark, and James Grant as the discreet aide, and Angela Pleasance as a beguiling sexpot. Pinter's direction is impeccably smooth and suave.' Francis King of *The Sunday Telegraph* pointed out the ambiguity and flummery of Pinter's writing, 'which make the head of the institution [the colonel] exclaim at one point: "Something is happening but I don't know what." (Any member of the cast or of the audience might be hard pushed to explain to him). As this barking martinet, Derek Newark gives a forceful performance — though one wonders how long his voice will survive the run.' An anonymous critic in the *Daily Express* gave a succinct opinion: 'Derek Newark turns in a fine comic performance as the head of a slightly sinister institution run by the Government for purposes that are never revealed. But the play is very silly—Monty Python with delusions of profundity.'

The Hothouse transferred to the West End and opened at the Ambassadors Theatre in Cambridge Circus on 25 June. In his second review of the play, John Barber considered it to be 'one of the funniest plays Harold Pinter has written... and it is impeccably cast. Derek Newark's paranoid soldier is matched by James Grant's sinister aide, Angela Pleasance's black-stockinged seductress, and Edward de Sousa's imperturbable man from the ministry..."

The *Londoner's Diary* of the *Evening Standard* 31 July ran an interesting piece on Derek's growing relationship with Harold Pinter:

> Actor Derek Newark, currently starring as the blustering Colonel Roote in Harold Pinter's *Hothouse* at the Ambassadors, is turning into something of a don. He has been selected by Open University to lecture on Pinter for its English drama course. The appointment is surprising because Newark has no qualifications as a lecturer, but he is, however, a firm friend of Pinter's and was handpicked by the playwright to act in *The Hothouse*.
>
> A former military man—he spent five years in the army before going to RADA in 1958. Newark now travels to Milton Keynes every Tuesday to give his lectures. 'I talk about how we rehearse, what Harold is like to work with. I tell anecdotes and sometimes act out scenes. Harold is very particular about everything. I once asked him why he was worried about my paraphrasing a speech and

he replied "Because I'm a better writer than you are." That's how paranoid he is about text changes.'

At the beginning of June, Derek was invited by David Aukin of Hampstead Theatre Productions Limited to invest some money in *The Hothouse*, and he coughed up £1,500 to help keep the show running. He asked me if I were interested enough to also invest but I declined the generous offer. Out of curiosity I asked Derek if Pinter was going to invest in his own creation? Derek said, no, he was not going to, 'on a point of principle' —whatever Pinteresque-reason that may have been. When the play ended its run on 20 September after 13 weeks, Derek received the fruits of his investment—a cheque for £1,101—a loss of £399.00. He also received a letter of apology from David Aukin:

Dear Derek,
You may have read in the press about the decision of our Landlord at the Ambassadors to terminate our Licence. As a result, the show came off last Saturday. The circumstances in which our Licence was terminated were, to say the least, highly unsatisfactory but we were not in a position to resist. The show had been playing below its Notice Figure, i.e. the Landlord had the right to terminate, but we were in fact doing much better than many other West End productions. We were therefore shocked to be told to leave without the customary discussions with the Landlord. May I thank you for your faith in the show and say how bitterly I regret its ending with the consequent loss of part of your investment.

BANG OUT OF ORDER!

No tears, no regrets. On 9 October 1980, Derek was invited to celebrate the marriage of Harold Pinter and Antonia Fraser and to enjoy a show business buffet supper at their home in Campden Hill Square, a meeting at which led to a screening of *The Hothouse* in March 1982 on BBC2 television, with Derek and the cast playing their original roles, with Pinter as director.

*****

In 1980, Derek also appeared in the TV version of the stage hit *Bedroom Farce* in his original role of Malcolm. He went to Israel to take part in the TV mini-series *Masada*, starring Peter O'Toole as the Roman commander laying siege to the Jewish fortified citadel under the leadership of Eleazar ben Ya'ir played by the American star Peter Strauss. The story, based on historical events, pits the engineering skill and military might of Rome against the passion and ingenuity of the besieged Jewish Zealots holding-out in Masada.

Derek played the Roman engineer officer in charge of building the siege machines and siege operations. He told me that he saw very little of the grand O'Toole on the sun-blasted location. When he did arrive, it was in a stretched air-cooled limousine equipped with a cocktail bar, to which, after shooting his scenes, he would quickly retire away from the heat and swarming flies. Others in the mini-epic included Barbara Carrera, Anthony Quayle, David Warner, Timothy West, and Christopher Biggins.

Other television jobs included the popular BBC2 comedy-drama *Private Schulz*, with Michael Elphick as the eponymous anti-hero German conman who is reluctantly pressed into service with the

SS counter-intelligence plan to swamp Britain with fake five-pound notes in order to destabilise our economy in World War Two. His lunatic commanding officer was played by Ian Richardson. Derek was placed behind the bar as Jack the Publican. He and Michael became good friends and drinking mates.

Derek returned to the warm confines of the Cottesloe to appear in Arthur Miller's 1953 classic *The Crucible* on 30 October 1980, playing the part of Thomas Putnam. The play about the witchcraft trials in Salem, Massachusetts in 1692 ran until 1 January 1981 after 40 performances. For most of 1981, Derek was engaged in television work. He was back at the Cottesloe in August to appear as Robolledo, a soldier, in *The Mayor of Zalamea* by Pedro Calderon de la Barca, directed by the distinguished Michael Bogdanov, known as 'the Bodger' to the irreverent Cottesloe troupe. Also in the cast was Derek's long-standing friend Daniel Massey, playing Captain don Alvaro de Ataide.

In 1981, Derek also featured in episodes of *Only Fools and Horses* and the police series *Juliet Bravo*. In 1982, Derek donned the swastika mantle of top Nazi Martin Bormann in the TV film production of *Inside the Third Reich*, where he was reunited with some colleagues from previous plays and films: George Murcell, an old mate, played Goering, David Shawyer was Himmler, and Maurice Roeves was Hess. Ian Holm played Goebbels, the Dutch actor Rutger Hauer was Albert Speer, Hitler's chief architect, and John Gielgud his aristocratic father. Derek Jacobi delivered a chilling, mesmerising study of Adolf Hitler. *Inside the Third Reich* was based on Speer's own memoirs with the same title published in 1970. The film was shot on location in Munich. Derek in uniform, with cropped hair and scar looked so remarkably like the real Bormann that, so Derek told me, a veteran Nazi acting as a consultant on the set, gaped in sudden awe and automatically clicked his heels at the 'phantom' figure standing before him.

While waiting around on set to be called before the camera, the principal actors played cards and talked show business. John Gielgud, a somewhat discreet homosexual of the old school, would often as not, kick-off the conversation with, 'Good Morning, gentlemen, and whom shall we bitch about today?'

Gielgud, known to his intimates and favoured cronies as 'Johnny Gee', had worked with Derek before on the film *Oh! What a Lovely War* (1969), and their paths had crossed many times in productions at the National Theatre where they occasionally drank together in the Green Room bar. In the future, they would both appear in the TV mini-series *War and Remembrance*, a sequel to the TV series *Winds of War* (1983) from the books by Herman Wouk.

John Arthur Gielgud was second only to Laurence Olivier in competition for the grand title of greatest British stage actor of the 20th century. He established his reputation in the 1930s as a master of classical roles. Olivier once said of him: 'John has a dignity, a majesty which suggests that he was born with a crown on his head.' Alec Guinness described Gielgud's voice as a 'silver trumpet muffled in silk'. Richard Burton praised him succinctly: 'He's the best bloody verse speaker in the world!' No other actor, it seems, could match him for elegance, sensitivity and intellect. He was knighted in 1953 and appointed to the Order of Merit in 1996.

During an off-camera conversation with Gielgud, Derek

casually mentioned the name of Harry Andrews (1911-1989), the gruff, jut-jawed, top-league supporting actor in many war and adventure films. Derek admired him for his authentic military characters. Andrews had joined the Royal Artillery at the very start of World War Two and served throughout the conflict reaching the rank of acting-major.

'I first met young Harry in 1935,' said Gielgud. 'He played Tybalt in my production of *Romeo and Juliet*. A few years later he appeared in a peculiar little show aptly-named *He Was Born Gay*... a singular situation of which I am sure you are aware Derek. Dear Harry never reached the higher realms of cinematic stardom because he refused plastic surgery to reduce his elephantine, sticking-out ears.'

For all his natural hauteur, Gielgud was, in many ways, an ingenuous and modest man who enjoyed gay gossip and rude stories. He was neither reticent nor coy about relating a self-mocking anecdote. He told Derek the following tale of personal mortification, which Derek took immense relish in re-relating to me (as he always did) in mellifluous mimicry of the great Johnny Gee.

Gielgud was invited by an aristocrat of long lineage to his vast stately pile. After a full and formal dinner, Sir John found himself alone late at night in his guest bedroom without an en suite lavatory. Suddenly, he was taken acutely short. He did not know where to find a loo in the ancient rambling mansion of many rooms. He had to relieve himself immediately.

'It was a force majeure I can assure you, Derek.' He placed a copy of the *Daily Telegraph* on the floor and, 'much to my utter shame, I shat on it.'

'I wrapped the turd in the paper,' Sir John continued, 'and placed the unfortunate package in a dark corner of an enormous Victorian wardrobe, intending to explain the sorry incident to my host in the morning. However, I left in a hurry without doing so.

'A year or so later, I was invited there again. By this time I had forgotten about the previous "accident". On leaving the place my driver handed me a wonderful gift-wrapped box, saying the elderly butler had mumbled something about Sir John having left something behind. When I opened the box I found my *Telegraph*-wrapped turd, now petrified, of course. I can assure you, Derek, the old aristocracy are indeed a breed apart.'

It was now Derek's turn to tell a story and he chose to entertain Sir John with the blasphemous 'true' tale of the nun and the cabbie. A middle-aged nun in full habit hailed a London taxi. On the journey the cab driver revealed a long-held inner desire.

'Forgive me, Sister, for saying this... I've always wanted to kiss a nun. It's a craving that's driving me insane!'

After a short silence the nun replied 'Are you a good Catholic? Are you a single man?'

The cabbie assured her that he was.

'Then park in a secluded spot,' said the nun. Having done so, the driver got into the back with his passenger. 'I think we can do better than a kiss,' said the nun.

She then unzipped his trousers and, with the pious invocation, 'May God forgive this sinful act of mercy,' she gave the utterly astonished cabbie a 'blow-job'.

On continuing the journey, the now agitated driver blurted out: 'I'm so sorry Sister but I lied to you—I'm not Catholic,

I'm Jewish and I'm married. May God forgive me for deceiving you. May I burn in Hell...'

The nun cut him short, and in a voice now deeper, said: 'Don't upset yourself cabbie. Calm down. I'm not a real nun, I'm an actor... my name's Richard and I'm on my way to a fancy dress ball!'

Derek also made me laugh by passing on another 'Johnny Gee' anecdote. Gielgud was walking through Leicester Square in 1954, accompanied by Noel Coward, the famous playwright and fellow homosexual. Coward was a fund of gay gossip and knew most of the secrets of the 'homo' demi-monde. The square housed several major cinemas, and the pair espied a huge poster advertising the film *The Sea Shall Not Have Them*, an RAF-Naval drama of World War Two starring the bisexual actor Michael Redgrave and the 'closet-queen' Dirk Bogarde.

The naughty Noel pointed at the poster, turned with a smile to Gielgud, and created a show business legend with his bitchy comment: 'The Sea Shall Not Have Them—I don't see why not... everybody else has!' Sir John Gielgud died in 2000 at the grand old age of 96.

Harold Pinter finally got his wish to see his grim and mysterious stage play, *The Hothouse*, on mainstream television. It was shown on BBC2, Saturday 27 March 1982 at primetime. Derek reprised his original role as Colonel Roote, as did the six other members of the original cast. Pinter directed and Louis Marks produced, the latter sent a note to Derek, saying, 'I'm sorry there has been such a long delay putting this play out, but part of the reason has been the need to find a special slot for what everyone acknowledges to be a very important production.'

BANG OUT OF ORDER!

In an interview with Robert Ottaway of the *Radio Times*, Pinter gave some background and reason for writing this extraordinary piece of fiction:

> Harold Pinter tells me, 'I found the play very funny. And the point I want to stress is that it was fantasy when I wrote it, but now it has become, I think, far more relevant. Reality has overtaken it.' Way back in the 50s, Pinter became a guinea pig in a psychiatric hospital, subjected to a test 'for ten bob a time'. And that was an experience, involving electrodes in the head, which has stayed with him ever since... 'In many ways,' he said. 'I'm happier with this TV version.' And that is perhaps because TV lends itself to the real rather than the imaginary... About the play itself, which I saw in the theatre. I can only underline the verdict of one critic, who said: 'It has the authentic frisson. We are obliged to laugh uproariously—but we feel utterly guilty about it.'

*****

Ten years after casting Derek in *Oh! What a Lovely War*, director Richard Attenborough delivered on his promise to work with him again. Putting together the cast for his historical epic *Gandhi*, he offered Derek a substantial role in the film and it seemed certain that he would take the part—it being mentioned as a news item in *The Londoner's Diary* of *The Evening Standard*:

> A remarkable piece of serendipity for Sir Richard Attenborough and his Gandhi film, currently shooting

in India. For the young actress who flies out today to play Edwina Mountbatten is, in fact, a relation of India's favourite Vicereine, Jane Myerson, 24... Miss Myerson will be joining the RSC's Ben Kingsley in the title role, and the National Theatre's Derek Newark for Attenborough's epic, which is budgeted at a tidy £8 million.

It seemed a chance in a million to further Derek's career. *Gandhi* made a global star of the virtually unknown Ben Kingsley, but Derek was riding high at the time. He had several decent film roles to his credit, one of them as Sean Connery's police partner, and he had just returned from the Broadway success of *Bedroom Farce*. However, negotiations broke down between Derek and Dickie; whether it was Derek's fault or that of his over-reaching agent has never been clear to me. It could have been a case of Derek's hubris, his self-inflation of his commercial worth. Whatever the reason, the upshot was that he out-priced himself on *Gandhi*. The often lachrymose 'luvvie' that he was, Attenborough could also be ruthlessly brief. He sent Derek an international telegram:

Dear Derek, devastated that you may not be able to be with us, but I fear that the proposed figure [fee] is way beyond our budget. Fondest regard, Dickie Attenborough.

And that was the end of the *Gandhi* offer. A grand missed opportunity. The film was released in 1982 to great acclaim. Ben Kingsley became an over-night international film star and 'dear Dickie' progressed to yet more epic movies.

In June 1982, Derek appeared as the Curate, Piero Perez,

in *Don Quixote* performed in The Olivier Theatre. The noble Paul Scofield commanded the stage as Don Quixote and Tony Haygarth his servant Sancho Panza. Adapted from Cervantes by Keith Dewhurst and directed by Bill Bryden, it ran for 56 performances. Derek's theatrical highlight of the year came with Bryden's bizarre conception and direction of Shakespeare's *A Midsummer Night's Dream* that opened on 25 November. Derek was cast as Nick Bottom, and his Cottesloe stage 'rival' Jack Shepherd as Puck. Paul Scofield played Oberon. In the event, Bryden's resolve to use Edwardian summer dress to preface the night with a brief medley of Edwardian music hall tunes did not meet with total approval. Robert Cushman of the Sunday *Observer* had this to say:

> The band strikes up *If It Wasn't for the Houses in Between*, and we wonder what that has to do with a wood near Athens, or near anywhere else. It then segues into *Lily of Laguna*, which is even more bemusing, and finally settles on *Beautiful Dreamer*, which makes sense… The clowns are led by Derek Newark's quietly self-confident Bottom and include a Snout by Tony Haygarth who, as Wall, drops delightful bricks.

Benedict Nightingale of *The New Statesman* considered 'Derek Newark, a Bottom with a social as well as histrionic ambitions and an ability to lift his accent from downstairs to upstairs (or at least halfway upstairs) at the turn of an internal switch, the National has found a splendidly downbeat comedian, all nudge, wink, and sly pomposity.' Sheridan Morley of *Punch*, said: 'Bottom—Derek

Newark in an excellently dour performance—and his mates do a Wilson, Keppel and Betty routine in the final court scene which is nothing short of hilarious.'

A Midsummer Night's Dream went on the road and opened at Bath's Theatre Royal on 29 November for eight performances only. Princess Margaret graced the first night to celebrate the re-opening of the century-old refurbished theatre after a three-year restoration project. Jeremy Fry, a wealthy Bath businessman and a close friend of the Princess, was the driving force behind the brilliant renovation. To a fanfare of bugles of the 6th Battalion Light Infantry, the Princess, wearing a full length turquoise gown with a white mink stole, took her seat between Mr Fry and the legendary choreographer Sir Frederick Ashton.

At the back-stage reception after the show, the smiling Princess praised Bill Bryden in person for such a 'magical evening' and was introduced to each member of the cast. As the party got underway and the drink flowed generously, former Guardsman Derek engaged the Princess in convivial conversation... then came the unfortunate clash of heads. Jack Shepherd witnessed the incident and recalled in his book, *Impossible Plays*—'The Princess dropped something on the floor, bending forward to pick it up at exactly the same time that Derek bent forward to do the same. Their heads collided... but I don't think this was the reason why he was thrown out of the party.'

After the royal 'head-butt' both participants resumed their amiable conversation, then Derek must have said something out of order, for it signalled a royal security man to step forward. And the next moment, Jack Shepherd stated, Derek was 'bundled out of the building in a most unceremonious fashion... his arm locked painfully behind his back, a security man murmuring in his ear, "be a brave soldier", as he was danced down the staircase on the tips of his toes and then propelled into the street below.'

Whatever Derek must have said to the Princess remains a secret, for he never confided in me. However, he did tell me that for a brief moment he had held an ashtray for the Princess while she smoked a cigarette, and therefore felt justified in claiming the unofficial post of 'Keeper of the Royal Ashtray'. A year later, Derek and the Princess were to meet again at a backstage party for the NT's production of *Cinderella*.

This particular production of the *Dream* lasted 35 performances—from 25 November 1982 to 2 June 1983. After a short tour it returned home for a continued run at the National. Jack Tinker the formidable 'Critic of the Year' of the *Daily Mail*, gave his mixed impressions of the first night at the Lyttelton Theatre: 'Only the prospect of Robert Stephens, that rare and dangerous actor, taking over [from Paul Scofield] as King of the Fairies could have led me willingly back to this tedious marathon *Dream*... The mechanicals [a dance team] helped to pass the time engagingly enough led by Derek Newark, who gives us a Bottom who is clearly more than a little under the spell of Tommy Cooper.'

*****

Much to his discredit, Derek continued to drive while under the influence of alcohol. He realised he was being a bloody fool but he did not stop his dangerous driving. After several minor shunts, and one serious incident on the way to perform at Brighton, he was finally brought to a London court in March 1982. After a late night drinking session in the Green Room, he was in a minor collision with a black cab. No injuries were incurred. Derek and the cabbie got out of their vehicles to talk, face to face. The cabbie accused Derek of being drunk. Derek admitted to having a few drinks but insisted that he wasn't incapable. He then cut short the conversation, got into his car and drove off.

The incensed cabbie contacted several other black cabs and, according to Derek, they all followed him to his Cottesloe colleague Tony Haygarth's mews cottage in central London, where Derek was staying the night. When he parked his car in the mews, Derek told me, all the cabs caught him in their concentrated headlights: 'I felt like a prisoner trying to escape'.

Alerted by the cabbie, the police arrived and tested Derek's alcohol level, found it well over the top, and this time he landed in court. I was there to witness his futile performance in the dock. His personal dialogue in defence was inept and bizarre in its twisted reasoning. There were moments when I had to suppress laughing out loud.

Instead of pleading guilty and throwing himself on the mercy of the court, he decided to ignore his defence counsel and, rather than show humility, was eager to brazen it out. He was Derek Newark. He would not be intimidated by the legal process. He would go down all guns blazing. He alienated the bench from the start with his unbridled arrogance. The cabbie had accused him of being drunk at the wheel, and threatening him with violence. Derek proposed the daft defence that the cabbie was lying: 'Me, threaten him with violence? Can you see the size of him? He's bigger than I am!' And he put forward the puerile notion that the cabbie was 'jealous' of his TV fame (Derek had starred in several recent crime series) and 'wanted to humiliate and deflate me'.

Dressed in a black overcoat, glaring at the court, Derek looked every inch a stage villain. 'It was'—he told the bench in all seriousness—'a classic case of "Gunfighter syndrome" in which the new "shootist" in town [meaning the cabbie] aspires to gun down the celebrated gunfighter [Derek] in order to establish a reputation...' It was pure John Wayne nonsense of course, but that's what he said—I was there. The wonder is that he kept a straight face while delivering this farcical codswallop.

When the young female prosecuting counsel said 'I put it to you Mr Newark that you were drunk and incapable in charge of a motor vehicle,' he cut her short.

'You can put it to me as much as you like, my dear,' he said. 'And I put it to you that, yes, I had a few drinks to alleviate the stress of a demanding performance. And I had a few more at Mr Haygarth's place. But I insist I wasn't drunk at the time of the collision.'

He was found guilty as charged, fined £400 and banned from driving for five years. As far as I can remember his counsel charged him £2000 and advised him to appeal, which he refused. Derek had his big day in court—and messed up his part with a forlorn display of hubris.

After the court case he never drove again. During the day he now had to take the train from Purley to Waterloo Station, thence to the National Theatre. But the train journey home, late at night, proved to be very inconvenient. So his hapless wife Jean was dragooned into service as his driver, motoring into crowded London every night to pick-up the tired and emotional Derek, and then the long and boring ride back with him always resounding off about some performance problem or other. They argued continuously about domestic issues. And when Jean became fully aware of Derek's serious and torrid affair with Elizabeth, their fragile, futile marriage came to a bitter end.

Elizabeth (Lizzie) was a convent-educated pretty little blonde Derek had met at some Soho pub or club. She was flirtatious and flippant, in her late twenties, Derek some twenty years older. He was proud of his new 'conquest'. In fact, the avaricious little minx had ensnared him. As far as I knew she had no qualifications, no career-plan, no regular job. She just needed a successful man to look after her as a kept woman. And he needed a lover. She was not the ideal companion for Derek at this critical stage in his declining years. Lizzie was a good-time girl who lived for today... bugger tomorrow. Both were tempestuous. They had violent arguments and, when in a drunken mood, he would physically assault her. Sex and money—his money—kept them together for some five years. When the acting jobs dried-up, his drinking increased, and the money was gone—she dumped him.

*****

In Derek's time at the NT the Green Room often seemed to resemble an international meeting place of the stars, with so many famous faces gathered there, together with those not so famous, and those yet to become famous. In 1980, Broadway actor and film star Stacey Keach could be seen at the bar, when working the lead in *Hughie*, a 1941 play by Eugene O'Neill, directed by Bill Bryden. At various times Robert de Niro, Al Pacino, and Dustin Hoffman brought a touch of Hollywood to the place. One would see Albert Finney, Michael Gambon, a young Jim Carter, an aspiring Tom Wilkinson, and a youthful Timothy Spall, and the little figure of Bob Hoskins. I was Derek's guest on many occasions and found it to be an exciting place to have a drink, rubbing elbows at the bar with all these actors. It was difficult not to appear star-struck in such company.

Harold Pinter, a part-time director at the NT, was not a regular drinker at the Green Room, but when he did enter the bar he usually sought out Derek. On one occasion, I found myself in a three-handed group with Pinter and Derek in full banter. Derek mentioned to the playwright that my son Tim had recently had a book published at the age of 18, to which Pinter mockingly replied, 'Is there no fucking end to the Newark family talent?' Derek just laughed, he had become inured to Pinter's sardonic comments. When I ventured to say that Pinter was a most unusual name, the great man said, 'Yes... there was a Hungarian sprinter named Pinter.'

He seemed to me a melancholy man; his conversation spiced with expletives. He was dressed formally in dark suit and necktie with heavy-rimmed glasses, a distinctive figure amid a crowd of scruffy actors, like a Bateman banker at the wrong convention. When the badinage turned to 'posh' establishments that don't let you in without a tie, Pinter related the following tall tale:

An Arab and his camel in the open desert... thirsty, in search of water... come upon a Jewish merchant with his stall decked with neckties. 'Can I sell you a tie?' he asks the Arab. 'No, I don't want a tie, infidel pig! I want water.' The merchant shrugs. 'Sorry, I don't have water to spare. My brother has a café, he's got plenty of water. His place is over there,' he points. 'Not far away'. The thirsty Arab rides in that direction. A little later he returns to the tie merchant, who asks, 'Did you get water?'—'No,' said the still thirsty Arab. 'The bastard infidel wouldn't let me in without a tie!'

Derek renewed his professional relationship with Pinter when rehearsals began in April 1983 for *The Trojan War Will Not Take Place*. The play, a 'prequel' to the Iliad, was written by Jean Giradoux in 1935 and originally entitled *Tiger at the Gate*; it was translated into English by Christopher Fry in 1955. Pinter had decided to direct it. He commanded a strong cast: Martin Jarvis as Hector the Trojan; Nicola Pagett as Helen of Troy; Barrie Foster as Ulysses the Greek—and Derek Newark as Ajax, the Greek King of Salamis.

The setting of the play is Troy before the outbreak of the Trojan War. Peace-loving Hector keeps repeating ironically that 'the Trojan War will not take place', eventually persuading Paris, who has abducted Helen, and even the willing but dubious Ulysses to cooperate in avoiding war. But the Trojans have been inflamed for various reasons, and it is finally not the leaders' decision, but the inevitable consequences of a warmonger's lie, that precipitates the war.

It was a difficult play to interpret. Rehearsals proved contentious and Pinter endured a 'rotten time' pulling the production together. During one heated moment Derek said something untoward and the fractious Pinter snapped: 'You're out of order, Derek... leave the room!' And on this rare occasion, the usually bullish ex-guardsman, dutifully obeyed his superior officer and left the room without further comment. The play— some two hours 45 minutes long— was not a success with the critics, who mostly blamed Pinter for its ponderous pace. It opened at the Lyttleton on 10 May and ran for 43 performances. Martin Jarvis was greatly surprised when Derek —not known for praising other actors—said to him, uninvited, 'You were bloody marvellous... marvellous... but never ask my opinion again.' A paradoxical compliment typical of Derek's complex character.

Kenneth Cranham, another NT acting colleague, received an altogether different kind of critical comment. Once, while standing in the wings with Derek, Cranham was all tensed-up, about to follow the great Albert Finney on stage, when Derek said to him: 'Trouble with Alby is he loses his bottle and rushes it... just like you do, Ken.'

'Not exactly the kind of encouragement I needed at that moment,' Cranham recalled with a laugh. He also retains a vivid memory of walking into the Green Room and seeing Derek standing at the bar in his full Ugly Sister drag (while appearing in *Cinderella*): awful blonde wig, lipstick and powder, false tits, having a lively difference of opinion with another actor. Derek with a large vodka gripped in his big, masculine mitt. Cranham was not privy to much of the conversation but he did catch Derek's memorable, mysterious line... 'When you've strangled a man in the jungle, then you can speak on equal terms...'

Having recreated the sardonic image and wit of Groucho Marx on the stage at the National Theatre, Derek added another long-held ambition to his repertoire of great cinema entertainers: WC Fields, in the TV play *Hollywood Hits Chiswick*, shown on Channel Four, 8 September 1983. In a special adaptation by Mike Sharland of his successful theatre presentation, Derek dominated centre stage as the legendary Fields. Produced by the Bright Thoughts Company, the play opens in Heaven, where Fields has been for 37 years... and now he wants to get out.

He chooses to return to the Chiswick Empire, scene of his first stage appearance in London as a top-rated juggler. But the Empire has been demolished and replaced with a supermarket, where Fields surveys the produce on sale: 'They're replacing live variety with dead vegetables.' Then, running a bibulous eye over the shelves crammed with liquor, 'Pon my soul, just like Heaven.'

Dressed in bowtie, straw boater, and smoking a cigar, Derek proved the very embodiment of the cinema comedian, relating his life story, accurate in tone of speech without being slavish. Fellow actor Christopher Timothy wrote Derek the following note: 'Dear Derek, Having just seen your WC Fields and you were bloody marvellous. Thanks—and continued success.' Malcolm Parkin, a dedicated and knowledgeable fan of Fields wrote to Derek care of The National Theatre:

> I simply have to write having just seen your incredible portrayal of WC Fields on TV. It was an absolute 'Tour de Force'. Never have I seen such accuracy of observation and brilliance of execution. Some passages

were uncanny in their feeling for the Great Man. I had thought Rod Steiger's version to be very high standard, but it doesn't stand up when compared to your own performance...please accept my thanks for a wonderful piece of work and my congratulations to you.

Derek again donned German uniform in 1983 as the Prussian General Stoessel in *Reilly: Ace of Spies*, an epic 12-part TV mini-series starring Sam Neill as Sidney Reilly, and based on the true exploits of British spy Reilly during and after World War One. The fine supporting cast included Leo McKern, Tom Bell, Kenneth Cranham, David Suchet, Peter Egan, and Ian Charleson. The following year Derek appeared as Detective Chief Superintendent Sullivan in six episodes of *The Travelling Man* series. And two episodes of *Just Good Friends* (1983-86) as the character Eddie Brown. He delivered an excellent portrayal of senior SS officer Theodore Eike in the TV special *Hitler's SS: Portrait of Evil*. Eike was a key member of the assassination squad that eliminated Hitler's Nazi rivals in the so-called 'Night of the Long Knives' in June 1934. A year later Derek appeared as Colonel Pietruska in *The Deliberate Death of a Polish Priest*.

*****

The next project on Derek's busy stage agenda for 1983 proved to be a significant one for him: *Glengarry Glen Ross*, a new play by David Mamet, a 35-year-old American born in Chicago. The play is set in a dodgy real estate office. Mamet himself worked for a short period in such an office in Chicago, and he describes the experience that led to writing the play:

BANG OUT OF ORDER!

The office was a fly-by-night operation which sold tracts of undeveloped land in Arizona and Florida [with misleading names like Glengarry Glen Ross] to gullible Chicagoens. The firm advertised on radio and TV and their pitch was to this effect: 'Get in on the ground floor... Beautiful home-sites in scenic/historic Arizona/Florida. For more information call... for our beautiful brochure.' Interested viewers would telephone in for the brochure and their names and numbers were given to me. My job was to call them back, assess their income and sales susceptibility, and arrange an appointment with them for one of the office salesmen.

This appointment was called a 'lead'... a lead being a 'prospect'. It was then my job to gauge the relative worth of these 'leads' and assign them to the sales force. The salesmen would then take their assigned 'leads' and go out on the appointments, which were called 'sits'— i.e. a meeting where one actually 'sits down' with the prospects. So that's the background to the play. We are in a real estate office. There is a sales contest near its end. The four salesmen have only several more days to establish their position on the sales graph, the 'board'. The top man wins a Cadillac, the second man wins a set of steak knives, the bottom two men get fired! The competition centres around the 'leads', with each man trying desperately to get the best ones.

David Mamet greatly admired Harold Pinter and sent him the

yet un-produced play. Pinter was immediately much impressed by the manuscript and sent copies to both Bill Bryden and Peter Hall; they also recognised the work as a masterpiece and accepted the play for production at the Cottesloe. Mamet came over and attended rehearsals and stayed on for previews—and theatrical triumph. Pinter, a constant advocate of the new play, also helped in rehearsals and with the production. Indeed, Mamet dedicated the play to Pinter. When Mamet considered the cast were not playing it ruthless enough in the unrelenting drive to induce, to brow-beat honest people into buying worthless land, he reproved them with, 'Listen... these guys, they could sell you cancer.'

The world premier of *Glengarry Glen Ross* opened at the Cottesloe Theatre on 21 September 1983. The leading members of the seven-man cast were, in the order of speaking: Derek Newark as Shelly Levene, Karl Johnson as John Williamson, Trevor Ray as Dave Moss, James Grant as George Aaronon, and Jack Shepherd as Richard Roma. Bill Bryden directed. Milton Shulman of *The Standard* attended the first night:

> Willy Loman in *Death of a Salesman* [by Arthur Miller] needed the New England territory to provide him with a living and give him dignity as a salesman. The salesmen in Glengarry Glen Ross... need 'leads' to enable them to make a hard buck...As the contest reaches its last days, the men anxiously try to increase their sales performance. Shelly Levene (Derek Newark) has been losing his selling ability and bribes the office manager (Karl Johnson) for some good leads... Derek Newark and

Trevor Ray impressively use their explosive, repetitive chatter to expose the bitterness beneath the confident exterior... Bill Bryden sensitively orchestrates this closed world of desperation and expectation at the bottom end of the American dream.

Michael Billington in *The Times* said: 'Derek Newark as the salesman on the skids also combines a bruising, militaristic ferocity with a lamb-like meekness at his final humiliation.' The growing 'rivalry' between Derek and Shepherd to be best actor in the show was becoming increasingly evident. Michael Coveney of the *Financial Times* observed that 'The pace of the evening is eventually controlled by Derek Newark's ebullient Shelly Levene and, especially, Jack Shepherd as his electrically quicksilver rival. Both do full justice to Mamet's skill of constructing a fabric of deviant, rhythmic "salespeak".' Michael Billington of *The Guardian* said 'I wouldn't class the play with *Death of a Salesman*... but what Mamet does show is how the fight for survival bends personal morality... there are riveting performances from Jack Shepherd as the white-suited hustler backing away from people as he gets more vocally aggressive. And from Derek Newark as a flannel-suited blusterer bullying the very man from whom he most needs help.'

As the play progressed to full-capacity audiences, it was generally recognised in the NT's Green Room bar that Derek was tipped to win an Olivier Award as best actor for his part in the show. He had been off the booze for several months. He had worked damned hard in the role. Everybody praised him. He wanted to win. And he was certain that he had done enough to bag the prize. But it was not a one-horse race—Jack Shepherd was there, his main rival, disputing the outcome.

In the event, *Glengarry* won the award for Best New Play... and Jack Shepherd took the award for Best Performance in a New Play. A bitterly disappointed Derek returned to his old drinking habit. But the show went on. *Glengarry* played to full houses at the Cottesloe until 20 March 1985 after 149 performances; it then transferred to London's Mermaid Theatre, where it ran until 10 May 1986, still under the direction of Bill Bryden. The only change in the original cast was that Kevin McNally replaced Jack Shepherd as Richard Roma.

The play won Mamet the American Pulitzer Prize and he went to Hollywood to adapt *Glengarry* for the screen. Directed by James Foley, it was released in 1992. The film boasted a stellar cast: Derek's role as Shelly Levene was played by Jack Lemmon, Jack Shepherd's part by Al Pacino, and the office manager by Kevin Spacey. All of them—like their Cottesloe precursors—gave brilliant ensemble performances. Derek had given his best-ever performance as Shelly Levene. Bill Bryden tells an anecdote about Michael Linner, who had been involved in the London production of the play. Having just seen the film, Linner said to Bryden: 'Who would have guessed that Derek Newark was a better actor than Jack Lemmon?'

CHAPTER 11
Worst Ever Performance

From Derek's best ever performance to his most dismal display of his acting talent—in the pantomime *Cinderella* that opened at the Lyttelton on 15 December 1983. Adapted by Bill Bryden and Trevor Ray and directed by Bryden, they put together authentic Victorian songs, text, and jokes to produce a visually enchanting production, but in cleaning out the bawdy contemporary elements of traditional pantomime, they delivered a sterilised sugar plum confection. In selecting Derek, and his drinking buddy Robert Stephens, to play the Ugly Sisters, Bryden made an error of judgement. At the time, however, it seemed a great idea. Both had reputations as Green Room jesters, *ergo* they would be funny on stage in hilarious drag costume and face makeup. But the pairing proved a minor disaster.

Both were uncomfortable as the Ugly Sisters and did little to hide the fact. Neither managed to create the proper camp and comic character required. Their wooden, lacklustre performance was bereft of any humour. They could not, or would not, capture the music-hall spirit of pantomime. 'This came as a surprise to the rest of us,' recalled Jack Shepherd, who was also in the show, 'since, off stage, they could be utterly outrageous.' Stephens himself later confessed in his memoirs *Knight Errant*—'I was ridiculous. I looked like an old tart, and I was desperately unfunny. I should have known by then that I was not an innately funny actor [on stage]. But I was less innately unfunny than Derek Newark.'

The critics had a fine time tearing the show to pieces. Robert Cushman of *The Observer* blamed the text: 'The couplets, which are almost constant, are not gorgeously awful, but just execrably limp. They imprison the actors; you can feel Derek Newark, Robert Stephens, Jack Shepherd and the others pining to get out and be funny, but to no avail.' James Fenton's review in *The Sunday Times*: 'Of Gloria and Euphoria, the two Ugly Sisters, the latter played by Robert Stephens, seems so unhappy as to have caused some strong sympathy in my party, but Derek Newark is a glorious Gloria.' Michael Billington of *The Guardian*: 'What the show lacks is a real outgoing earthy comic presence. Derek Newark and Robert Stephens as the Ugly Sisters have the outlandish gear but insufficient aggression.' Martin Hoyle in *Plays and Players* was unimpressed: 'The chief offenders were the Ugly Sisters who evidently felt that slap and drag were enough to get by on without team-work or interest in the audience.'

Clive Hirschorn of the *Sunday Express* reported that 'only Tony Haygarth, the most endearing Buttons I have ever seen, fulfilled the requirements of traditional panto.' *The Spectator* reviewer agreed: 'the Ugly Sisters, Robert Stephens—morose and miserable; Derek Newark—spiteful and petulant. Tony Haygarth gives the best performance as Buttons.' Charlotte Keatley in her review concurred, 'the saving grace is Tony

Haygarth as Buttons, who is both moving and funny, and draws on techniques which go back the Grimaldi [the great pantomime clown 1779-1837].'

Princess Margaret, that ardent show-goer, attended a charity performance of *Cinderella* and afterwards joined the cast at a celebration party at *Maxim's* restaurant where she renewed her acquaintance with the 'Keeper of the Royal Ashtray'. Derek had learned his lesson. This time, his nearness to her Highness was the essence of discretion; not a word nor gesture out of order. The Princess, always proud of her knowledge of cockney culture, joined in with the others singing old music-hall songs round the piano until three in the morning. One tabloid paper reported it as a 'right Royal knees-up'.

Cinderella was an expensive production to stage and proved to be a critical and commercial flop. The critics disliked it and the public failed to patronise the show. It closed on 10 March 1984 after 90 performances. It's interesting to note that Bryden's original casting for the project first mooted in 1978 had been John Gielgud and Laurence Olivier as the Ugly Sisters! The miscarriage of *Cinderella* compounded the resounding failure of the NT's Marvin Hamlisch musical *Jean Seberg*, directed by Peter Hall, that ran concurrently at the Olivier Theatre with *Cinderella* at the Lyttelton for 75 performances; a production that went some £130,000 over budget. *Cinderella* proved to be the most damaging single factor in the year's deficit of £268,000. A dejected Peter Hall apologised to the NT board for 'bad luck and some misjudgement'.

When not in the heavy drag of an Ugly Sister, Derek gave fraternal support as stage director to his friend Bob

Hoskins, who had written a play called *All for the Nation*, that was presented at the Cottesloe as an early evening platform performance in February and March. It starred Robert Stephens, Robert Oates and Hoskins himself under the coy programme credit of 'A Bloke'. 'I've always written since I was a kid, poetry and stuff,' said Hoskins. 'I write very quickly to get it done. It would never be a full-time career. It's too lonely.' He had worked in Cambridge and Paris under the pseudonym 'Robert Williams'—'As I don't want to admit I'm responsible in case it's a load of rubbish. But as it's a bunch of mates doing the play this time, I can't really deny it.'

In April 1984, Derek again volunteered his support, both moral and physical, to a new playwright/actor named Bernard Sharpe. His play was called the *Last Decathlon* and set in three acts in an army gymnasium in Gibraltar in 1982. Derek's part as the physical training instructor, seemed handmade for him and he attacked the role with relish. It was staged in the NT's Studio Two workshop. A two-man play with Sharpe as Sergeant Bartlett, known as 'Flexy' to his long-standing mate Staff Sergeant Hale (Derek), the PT instructor nicknamed 'Stormy'. As a mark of their friendship they had exchanged tattoos.

In Act One, Hale is drilling Bartlett into super fit condition for the annual army decathlon. When Bartlett's new wife suggests there's an element of homosexuality between the two men, Hale responds by nearly killing his mate. Bartlett, having succumbed to his wife's wishes, withdraws from the decathlon and is then called for service in the Falklands War. He returns six months later with his arm blown off; his wife leaves him, but Hale welcomes him back with gladness. In his review,

BANG OUT OF ORDER!

Roy Robert Smith regarded the play a 'glorious two-hander directed with agility by Jamie Dworin... Sharpe and Newark are a sympathetic duo. Newark's straightforward, rowdy, non-nonsense approach grapples splendidly with Sharpe's version of a man in a dangerous corner.' Bernard Sharpe sent a handwritten letter of gratitude to his co-actor:

> Dear Derek,
> One week and 25 torn-up pages later, I'm still trying to find the best way to say thanks so you'll know I mean it. It's a lot more than thanks for the *Last Decathlon* and your amazing Hale, it's more than your generous help to me as an actor and writer. Well, perhaps Bartlett says it best: 'You might not want to understand or believe but you are my mate!' You really are. Thanks & love, Bernard.

Derek's next prominent role in a play came in *Golden Boy*, a boxing drama staged at the Lyttelton in May 1984. He played Tom Moody, manager of a young Italian-American lightweight fighter named Joe Bonaparte. Written by Clifford Odets and first performed in 1937, *Golden Boy* tells the simple story of a young man's dilemma: should he continue to train and perform on the violin, in which he is gifted, or should he discard the violin and seek swifter success and fortune in the square ring, in which he is also highly proficient? Against his father's wishes, he chooses the ring. He yearns for early fame and fast cars. On the way, he steals the affections of his manager's girlfriend, and they both die in a car crash.

Golden Boy opened in New York in 1937 and then London in

1938. A financial triumph it bankrolled Odets' Group Theatre until America entered World War Two. Odets, a socialist with communist sympathies, uses the boxing world as a clumsy metaphor to knock the idealised concept of the so-called 'American Dream'. He subtitled *Golden Boy* a modern allegory of a greedy, corrupt and ruthless system; a competitive society that atrophies the soul.

Bill Bryden, an ardent boxing fan, was instrumental in bringing *Golden Boy* to the National. He found a new talent in Jeremy Flynn to play Joe Bonaparte and sent him for rigorous boxing instruction to the London gym of famous trainer Terry Lawless, who also served as the play's consultant. Derek played Tom Moody, Joe's manager. Jack Shepherd got the plum part of Eddie Fuseli, the sinister homosexual gangster who wants to 'buy a piece' of young Bonaparte.

Bryden's production opened at the Lyttelton Theatre on 22 May 1984. Milton Shulman of *The Standard* was at the first night:

> Clifford Odets made his reputation in the 1930s in America writing angry plays claiming that money corrupts the soul. He lost his reputation after the war when he went to Hollywood, apparently happy to be so corrupted... Although we never actually see a fight [on stage], we are kept on tenterhooks in the dressing room as the crowd's roar indicates the excitement of what is going on in the stadium. Jeremy Flynn is exceptionally good as the morose, troubled, aggressive Bonaparte... while Derek Newark has the crushed realism of a manager who has been in the game too long.

It was not only the acting that impressed the critics but the atmospheric set designs created by Hayden Griffin. Irving Wardle of *The Times* had this to say: 'It has been said before, but this production compels me yet again to salute Bill Bryden and his company as the most fruitful working group to have emerged in the National Theatre since its move to the South Bank... Performances like Derek Newark's small-time manager and his long-term girlfriend (shades of Nathan Detroit and Miss Adelaide from *Guys and Dolls*) have the precise bruised, nail-biting realism of people who have suffered a lifetime of disappointments but are fighting on for lack of any alternative.' Sean French in his *Vogue* magazine review said: 'Derek Newark's portrayal of Bonaparte's manager Tom Moody is a worthy addition to the repertoire of embittered, ulcerated losers that Bryden has assigned to him.' Stephen Fender in the *Times Literary Supplement*: 'Derek Newark makes the most of Moody's apparently motiveless aggression playing the full range and moving to mime the character's manic behaviour.'

Jack Shepherd—Derek's regular rival for best roles in Bryden's troupe—relates in his book *Impossible Plays* that 'Derek Newark was again well cast as Moody, the fight manager. This was one of his most accomplished performances and his last leading role with the company before the sad decline of his later years.'

Derek ended his constant, long-standing employment with the National Theatre on 20 April 1985. He had signed his first NT contract on 27 October 1975. His departure was caused by savage Government cutbacks in financial support and consequently the curtailment of the NT's activities. The Cottesloe was closed down for some six months; the last performance there was *Doomsday*—the final part of Bill Bryden's production of *The Mysteries*, all of which transferred to the restored Lyceum, the first live theatre to be staged there in 30 years.

The Mysteries—a modern version of the English Medieval Mystery Plays: the Nativity, The Passion, Doomsday—opened at the Lyceum on 18 May and ran until 3 August 1985. It fielded a cast of 21 characters with the actors taking more than one role. Derek, for example, played Abraham and First Soldier. The Cottesloe re-opened and continued operating under its original name for another 30 years. The space was then refurbished, reconstructed, and re-titled. Sponsored by Loyd Dorfman, founder and chief executive of the global business company Travelex, the old Cottesloe home opened as the new Dorfman Theatre in 2014.

It was during the performance of *The Mysteries* that an infamous boozing incident occurred. Drinking was so endemic with the Cottesloe crew that they would often imbibe just before a performance. Mostly they got away with it on stage, sometimes things went awry. During a performance of *The Passion* (part of the medieval *Mystery* plays), Mark McManus was cast as Jesus and Derek as one of four Roman soldiers. All five had been drinking freely in the Green Room and were well 'marinated' by the time they staggered on stage. They managed the dialogue without mishap, but their physical co-ordination was found wanting when attempting to haul Jesus aloft on the cross: they had to insert the base of the heavy cross into a floor socket that would hold it upright. As the four 'pissed' soldiers struggled to insert the base, the cross swung about dangerously... and it seemed that Jesus would crash headlong into the gasping audience—one of whom was Lindsay Anderson, the distinguished director.

Anderson, outraged at the impending disaster, rushed along the balcony that connected the theatre to the Green Room to protest to the other actors standing at the bar awaiting their final entrance. Jack Shepherd witnessed the incident. The indignant Anderson blurted out: 'Those men are drunk! All four of them... so drunk they can't get the bloody cross up. They're going to kill someone before they're done... and what makes it worse, the man playing Jesus—is even more drunk than they are!'

*****

After a sad farewell to the loyal Bill Bryden and his Cottesloe chums, Derek concentrated on getting more film and TV work in the following years, albeit taking on stage parts when they presented themselves.

In September 1987, Derek, in company with Timothy West, Peter Vaughan, and Jim Carter appeared in *Harry's Kingdom*, an award-winning play by Ron Pearson, about the 'cut-throat' world of double-glazing salesmen and their unsparing determination to be top of the team. To Derek, it brought back memories of his part in the stage play *Glengarry Glen Ross* in 1983, when he played an American real estate salesman. Timothy West had the role of Harry King, ruthless head of King Double Glazing. Derek was salesman Bob Roberts.

That same year saw the general release of the British feature film *Bellman and True*, in which Derek had second billing to Bernard Hill. A crime thriller, it told the story of computer expert Hiller (Hill) who gets coerced into helping a gang of crooks rob a bank using Hiller's electronic devices. Derek was perfectly cast as the nasty gang boss known only as the Guv'nor. He is particularly frightening when he threatens and intimidates Hiller by shoving a sawn-off shotgun in his back. Directed by Richard Loncraine and based on the novel by Desmond Lowden, its tightly-written screenplay contains gritty dialogue and a tragicomic break-in sequence where the Guv'nor reproves his less than efficient henchmen: 'It would be nice for my reputation if—at least—we got into the bank before we got nicked.' The film ends with Hiller outwitting the gang and blowing them all to kingdom come with a clever device while he escapes to safety.

It was Derek's last independent feature film role.

Derek was still in demand by TV producers. In 1988, he appeared in *A Taste of Death*, a six-part series produced by Anglia Television. An adaptation of a crime story by the popular novelist PD James, it starred Roy Marsden as detective hero Adam Dalgliesh, and a distinguished supporting cast of Simon Ward, Dame Wendy Hiller, Fiona Fullerton, Bosco Hogan, and Derek Newark as Gordon Halliwell, a tough, ex-sergeant major, now chauffeur to top Government minister Sir Paul Berowne, played by Hogan. Taciturn and secretive, Halliwell does not like his boss Berowne but his loyalty to certain members of the Berowne family is unswerving throughout the murder investigation. Anglia Television sold *A Taste for Death* for screening in the USA in a programme package worth a million dollars. That same year another lucrative mini-series came Derek's way in the shape of *War and Remembrance* that starred Robert Mitchum and Jane Seymour, in which Derek played the detestable Untersturmfuhrer Klinger, commandant of Auschwitz concentration camp.

In the summer of 1989, Michael Winner was casting for supporting actors for his comedy-crime movie *Bullseye!* starring Michael Caine and Roger Moore (both close friends of Winner). He called in Derek to consider him for the part of policeman Inspector Grosse. Derek was drinking heavily at this period and apparently he must have said something out of order that upset Winner. Derek didn't get the part—which went to his old film rival Derren Nesbitt! The film, released in 1990, turned out to be an absolute stinker, both critically and at the box-office. It is listed in the *Radio Times Guide to Films* as 'A hideously unfunny comedy of errors from Michael Winner that must rank as a career low for nearly all involved... an awful script.'

Despite his increasing drinking problem, Derek remained busy throughout 1989. In January, he appeared as a regular character, Mr Bennett, a blue-blazered club bore, in a new sitcom written by Johnny Speight called *The Nineteenth Hole*, starring Eric Sykes, about the so-called 'hilarious' chauvinistic events in a private golf club. It was not a success and was cancelled after a short run. Derek did not shine in the show.

In May 1989, Derek appeared at the Theatre Museum in London's Tavistock Street to give a lecture and share his knowledge and wealth of experience in the museum's *Shakespeare Week*. He received the following letter of thanks from the museum's curator Alexander Schouvaloff:

BANG OUT OF ORDER!

Dear Mr Newark,
On behalf of us all at the Theatre Museum may I thank you most sincerely for your generous participation in our recent successful 'Shakespeare Week'. We were thrilled indeed to welcome you here and extremely grateful to you for sparing your time and giving so much pleasure to so many people.

In August, he filmed an episode of the popular cop series *The Bill* produced by Thames Television, in a segment called *Greig Versus Taylor*. His work was appreciated by its director, Clive Fleury, who sent Derek a note:

Thank you very much indeed for all the effort you put into your characterisation of 'Eric Taylor'. We are now at the editing stage and everything seems to be going very well indeed... It was a difficult part to do without rehearsal, and your expertise and professionalism were greatly appreciated.

Derek received a follow-up thank you from producer Michael Simpson: 'Just a note of appreciation for your work on *Greig Vs Taylor* now it has been cut and dubbed. It was a great success with the Executive Producer himself, and the police who helped with advice on interrogation techniques, said it was a classic... I am very proud of you and the show.' In September, Derek briefly joined the *Paradise Club* for one episode of the crime series filmed by Zenith Productions, starring Leslie Grantham as the anti-hero Danny Kane. And thereby hangs a tale of true-life murder.

BANG OUT OF ORDER!

While serving as a regular in the Royal Fusiliers (the same London regiment that endured the Kray Twins) in West Germany in 1966, Grantham, then 19 years old, attempted to rob taxi driver Felix Reese at gunpoint. In the ensuing struggle, Reese died of a gunshot wound to the head. Grantham claimed he did not know the gun was loaded. He was found guilty of murder and sentenced to life imprisonment in 1967. He served ten years in various UK jails and was released in 1977. While in Leyhill prison, he acted in several plays to entertain inmates and members of the public. He was encouraged to make acting his career and in 1984 got his big break in the new soap opera *EastEnders* as the Queen Vic pub landlord 'Dirty Den' Watts. Soon after his first appearance, the *Daily Mirror* broke the story of his murky past. Nevertheless, he remained a popular character in *EastEnders* until February 1989.

Derek and Leslie developed an affinity. They drank together, exchanging army experiences and shared opinions on their chosen profession. Leslie respected classically trained actors like Derek. He considered himself something of an outsider in the 'acting game', a 'chancer' singularly lucky in having achieved TV stardom in such a short time. Derek, who could be pompous where acting as an art is concerned, empathised with Leslie's plain speaking and his straightforward, non-nonsense approach to the business. And Derek, being the emotional 'drama queen' that he sometimes could be, imagined that he saw in Grantham's former self as teenage killer, shades of Private Varley, the troubled soldier he portrayed so well in *End of Conflict*, all those years ago.

When Derek completed his stint in *The Paradise Club*, Leslie

Grantham expressed his hope that they would work together in the future. And they did. In 1994 Grantham was doing another crime series on ITV called *99-1* in which he played undercover cop Raynor. Derek was brought in for the episode *Where the Money Is* as gangster George Hicks, doing time for past crimes. In the convoluted plot in which Hicks escapes from custody while attending a funeral and then goes in search of hidden crime money, it is clear to all who knew Derek that he was in bad shape at this time. His injured right knee was giving him grief and, in order to run away from his guards in an opening sequence, he had his knee double-strapped and took some painkillers. But his disability was apparent. He was quickly out of breath, his knee gave way, and he ended up wheezing and puffing and swearing with pain. Physically, he was clearly at the end of his tether as an 'action man'.

*****

Derek returned to the boards in the spring of 1990, appearing in a leading role in Arthur Miller's play *The Price* at the Drum Theatre in Plymouth. It told the tale of two brothers—Derek and Ken Bones—who meet after many years apart to dispose of the contents of the family home; every dustsheet peeled back reveals a poignant memory and re-opens an old wound. Gabrielle O'Neill of the *Western Morning News* gave this review: 'Derek Newark is a sympathetic Victor Franz, convincing as the honourable policeman who is too straight-forward and straight-dealing to win in materialistic society. Ken Bones is an excellent foil as Walter Franz, the dapper doctor brother, smarter and sharper in business but with old resentments and neuroses of his own.'

Derek had established a solid reputation as an actor of quality—a versatile and dependable player—but his heavy drinking and consequential bad behaviour continued unabated. Indeed, it increased. We had a terrible row caused by his drinking and we did not speak for over a year. Alcohol eventually diminished his stage ability. His memory began to fail. He forgot his lines and proper gestures. An actor afflicted by that flawed faculty is facing the end of his career. And so it was with Derek. After his part in *The Price*, he appeared in August 1990 as Winston Churchill in the wartime drama *Soldiers*, a highly controversial play by the German polemicist Rolf Hochhuth.

The play, translated by Robert David MacDonald, portrayed Churchill as being involved in the 'assassination' of General Sikorski, the Polish leader killed in an air crash in 1943, thus contradicting the official report that it had been an accident. In short, Hochhuth claimed that Sikorski had been murdered on Churchill's orders. The play was due for production by the National Theatre in 1967 and, despite vigorous support by Kenneth Tynan, then the NT's literary manager, and Laurence Olivier, it was stopped dead by the NT Board led by its Chairman Lord Chandos—Chandos (then Oliver Lyttelton) had been a member of Churchill's wartime cabinet. The play was staged in the West End with John Colicos as Churchill in 1968.

When Hochhuth wrote the play, he was unaware that the pilot of Sikorski's Liberator plane, named Prchal, had survived the crash on take-off from Gibraltar. In the play Hochhuth had accused the pilot of participating in the assassination plot. So bad luck for the playwright that the very-much alive pilot sued Hochhuth for libel in the London courts. The maligned man won his case and was awarded £50,000 in damages and costs. Hochhuth to his great discredit fled to Switzerland to avoid payment. The scandal seriously affected the London theatre that had staged the play, and the theatre agreed to an out-of-court settlement.

Sponsored by Mercury Communications, funded by the Arts Council, and presented by Co-Producers in association with Theatr Clwyd, the 1990 production opened at Theatr Clwyd at Mold in Flintshire on 17 August for one week only, then on tour to Buxton, Brighton, Leeds, and finally London's Playhouse Theatre. At first, Derek was very good in the part, the embodiment of the bulldog Churchill, and received favourable reviews. But drink brought him down. He began to forget his lines. He was a mess. He suffered an alcoholic-induced breakdown. And to his utter shame and ever-lasting regret he walked out of the play during its London run.

The show was cancelled, he had no understudy, and there was talk of the theatre, or somebody, suing Derek for breach of contract, but nothing legal came of the affair. The professional ignominy remained indelible. Derek had broken his own rigid rule of theatrical conduct. Over the good years he was always hectoring his peers: 'As far as I'm concerned you can drink as much as you can take off stage—but when you walk out to do the business, that's where it counts... and what you never, ever do is let the team down ... You never lose your bottle.' Well, he did let the team down. He was bang out of order. And he never really recovered from the personal dishonour. He never worked in the theatre again. He was 57 years old.

Then, in February 1991, came further misfortune. He fell

heavily in a drunken state and seriously injured his neck. In hospital, they clamped a metal frame over his head and neck in order for the bones to mend. The contraption forced him on the wagon and he did not drink for several months. He did not work for a year or more. When he had fully recovered, he managed to pull himself together and appeared in several episodes of *The Bill*, one of which was called *Cutting Edge*. Despite his hapless condition, he proved that he had not lost all his old skills, as the following note of approval, dated 18 October 1993, from producer Michael Simpson affirms:

Dear Derek
I am writing to thank you for your work in 'Cutting Edge'. I thought you were very good, but the nice news is so did everyone else. It was both funny and touching and you gauged that last line perfectly. In fact we're breaking a *Bill* rule in employing you instead of a policeman!
All my thanks, as ever, Michael.

Around this time Derek and I were having lunch at the *Ivy* restaurant, the so-called 'Venue of the Stars'. He had been greeted and acknowledged by several well-known actors and seemed pleased with the 'professional' ambience. Then Michael Winner swaggered in with a female companion and sat at his usual table. After much deliberation as to whether he should or should not go over and say 'hello' to Winner, he did—and much to his chagrin, the seemingly agreeable Winner gave him a kind of dismissive 'push-away handshake' that Derek was all too familiar with, having used the subtle ploy himself to deter over-enthusiastic fans from further discourse.

He came back to me and said bitterly: 'Arrogant arsehole! Treating me like some star-fucked nobody... he knows who I am... I've been on Broadway... I've worked with Pinter for chrissake...' As you can imagine, it was not a pleasant lunch. But the food was good.

It was not to be Derek's last connection with Winner, who, in 1993 was presenting a London Weekend Television series called *Michael Winner's True Crimes*, a documentary-style production that reviewed notorious cases and the police investigation of the crimes committed. Winner neither directed nor produced the show; he had no influence in the casting of characters, he was simply the front-man presenter. On this occasion, the case re-visited was the 1984 IRA bombing of the Grand Hotel at Brighton, where Prime Minister Margaret Thatcher and her Cabinet were staying during the Conservative party conference. And Derek was chosen to play the senior investigating detective on the spot. He delivered a very credible performance.

The series gave birth to Winner's lasting dislike and contempt for his erstwhile show business friend Michael Grade, who at this time was a powerful and influential figure in television production. As head of Channel 4, Grade gave a speech at the Edinburgh Television Festival in which he condemned *Michael Winner's True Crimes* as the sort of programme that should not be on television, as it was exploitative and irresponsible. Winner felt betrayed and disgusted at Grade's unwarranted outburst, the result of which was that further production of *True Crimes* was cancelled. Winner never forgave his TV rival, citing Grade's motive as jealousy of what was a successful series that did not involve Channel 4.

At the age of 61, acting parts for Derek were few and far between. He did a BBC Radio reading of *The Haunting of Mahler*. His diminished physicality was such that he had to reject one TV commercial that called for him, and another mature actor, wearing grey wigs and beards and leaning on walking-sticks, to foment an argument and then suddenly change from doddery old boys into energetic 'sword-fencers' with their walking-sticks in the swashbuckling style of Errol Flynn. He was not fit enough for the stunt and had to pass on the job (it did not go to Derren Nesbitt). It brought down the final curtain on Derek's 30-year career in films and television. He would now live out the rest of his years surviving on state benefits and charity. He continued drinking to the very end.

CHAPTER 12
The Soho Scene

Outside the purlieu of the National, Derek patronised a small number of chosen drinking places. Soho was a favourite haunt: the *York Minster* pub in Dean Street, known to regulars as *The French*, and the *Coach and Horses* pub in Romilly Street, known to locals as 'Norman's gaff', after its obnoxious owner Norman Balon, dubbed by the press as 'the rudest landlord in Soho'. There were two afternoon drinking dens that Derek favoured: *Gerry's Club* also in Dean Street, and the *Kismet Club* in Little Newport Street, opposite the Arts Theatre. He rarely used the infamous and seedy but popular *Colony Room Club* in Dean Street, because he greatly disliked Muriel Belcher, its bitchy foul-mouthed lesbian owner, and her gay, wicked-tongued barman Ian Board. These pubs and clubs attracted a motley crowd of actors and writers and notable characters.

The French was so-named because its colourful landlord for many years was Gaston Berlemont, who sported a magnificent moustache. His Gallic charm and foreign moniker gave the impression he was French-born. In fact he first saw the light of day in Soho in 1914. His father, Victor Berlemont, a Belgian immigrant, founded the wine bar *Maison Berlemont* that later became the *York Minster* public house; legend has it that Gaston was born in an upper room. During World War Two, the pub was patronised by Free French servicemen and women. It is claimed that General De Gaulle composed his famous rallying call—'*A Touts Les Francais*'—in the upstairs restaurant of the pub, a copy of which still hangs in *The French*. The pub has always attracted a Bohemian clientele.

One early evening in 1973, Derek and I were standing at the bar of *The French*, which was full of regulars and tourists. Derek moved away to exchange banter with a small group of mates that included the actor Tom Baker, the scar-faced villain turned author Frank Norman, and his journalist colleague Jeffery Bernard. I stood at the bar, seemingly alone.

'You English, boyo?' enquired a Welsh voice at my elbow.

'Yes,' I replied.

'You live 'ere in London?'

Again I said 'yes'.

Then his smirking mate joined in.

'I feel sorry for you, boyo, living in a shit-hole like this!'

I turned to size up the two liberty-taking Welshmen. They were burly with beer-bellies, possibly up for some rugby game at Twickenham and now enjoying a drink and some English-baiting fun in sinful Soho. I decided to ignore the studied insult and turned my back on them. But they continued.

'London's the arsehole of England,' said one

'And unwiped, at that,' said the other.

My anger was rising. This was clearly a practised routine. They were cocky and confident in selecting a lone, easy victim. Suddenly, Derek's impressive bulk was at my side. He seemed to have sensed trouble brewing. I told him, *sotto voce*, what had transpired.

'I'll sort this out,' he said. In a magical instant he adopted his Cockney hard man persona. He straightened himself to full height. He was forty years old, still physically fit and fearless. He addressed them both.

'You taking the piss outta my bruvver! You better apologize... drink up and shove off— or I'll drag you both outside and do you serious damage!'

The Welsh windbags suddenly realised they had baited not only a soft touch but a Cockney toughguy.

'We're just joking, boyo... where's your sense of 'umour?'

Derek glared at them stony-faced. Just then Frank Norman brought his menacing scar-face into focus.

"Aving a bit of bovver, Derek?'

'Nuffink I can't 'andle, Frank.'

'OK. Call me if you need me,' and he moved off.

By now, the two blowhards were fast losing their bottle. Derek warned them again.

'Better apologize and fuck off, before I get really angry.'

They surrendered.

'Sorry, boyo, only joking,' and they quickly left.

As they walked away, I couldn't resist a parting shot: 'Picked a wrong'un this time, boyos!' And we laughed at their departure. It was Derek at his very best. Part actor, part the real man.

On another occasion in the crowded *French*, Derek and I were standing at one end of the bar, and Francis Bacon and Daniel Farson at the other end. Glances of recognition were exchanged. Derek was becoming a 'face' in Soho. After a little while Farson made his way over to us.

'My name's Daniel Farson... You're Derek Newark. Making your mark at the Royal Court, I hear. You're ex-Guardsman, I believe?'

Derek clicked his heels in mock attention.

'Coldstream, 2nd Battalion!' he snapped.

'Would you like a drink?' Farson asked. 'No, we're all right, we've got one,' said Derek, not wishing to encourage the man whose reputation as a homosexual was well known in Soho.

Farson ignored the brush-off and continued his patter.

'I interviewed a senior Guards officer once who, off camera, said to me: "There are too many fairies at the bottom of my Guardsmen."' And Farson laughed at the facetious play on words of Rose Fyleman's famous phrase.

Derek was not amused, but Farson pressed on.

'My friend, the eminent artist over there,' he pointed to Francis Bacon, 'would very much like to meet you.'

By now, Derek had had enough of the 'iron-hoof' banter. 'Tell you're painter mate that not all Guardsmen are queer. Tell him I'm a non-smoker and I don't need a fag! Now bugger-off to your mate who looks like a chipmunk.'

That was a reference to Bacon's prominent cheeks. I was quite surprised by Derek's turn of wit. Farson smirked acknowledgment at the bitchy retort and rejoined Bacon who, on hearing Farson's comment, raised his champagne glass towards Derek and called out a jovial 'Bravo!'

*****

BANG OUT OF ORDER!

The *Colony Room* was a single, first floor, front room overlooking Dean Street, the same crowded Soho street that housed the nearby *French* pub and *Gerry's Club*. Entrance was made by way of a narrow, shabby staircase and through a nondescript door, which opened on to a small room with a bar and an upright piano; not enough space for a baby grand. Muriel Belcher would be sitting on her usual bar stool, unsmiling, smoking a cigarette, scanning the denizens entering her private domain. She opened the club in 1948. Francis Bacon, then a young painter unknown to the general public and short of funds, was an early member. The bisexual Belcher always referred to the overtly homosexual Bacon as her 'daughter'. She made him an offer he could hardly refuse: 'I'll give you ten pounds a week and free drinks. Just bring in punters with money to spend.'

Bacon already knew lots of wealthy people and he introduced them to the new Soho watering-hole. The club soon became a favourite afternoon venue with both the boozy bohemian crowd and the rich and famous who enjoyed a drink on the wild side. Over the years, its membership became too numerous, too eclectic to mention in detail. Ironically, Bacon himself, eventually became the club's most famous and richest member, spending his increasing fortune generously on champagne for his admiring cronies, often with his celebrated toast: 'Champagne for my real friends—Real pain for my sham friends!'

The club became known to regulars as 'Muriel's'—just as the nearby *Coach and Horses* pub was called 'Norman's' after its loud-mouthed landlord. Muriel was pale and sharp-faced with a raptor's beak of a nose, her black hair pulled back severely. Bacon considered her bewitchingly beautiful and painted her several times, as did his friend and fellow-member Lucian Freud. She was celebrated for her quick 'camp' wit and acid tongue. She was aided and abetted by her gay barman and lieutenant, the foul-mouthed and bitchy Ian Board. Muriel had the ingrained habit of addressing all male members as 'Miss' or 'Mrs' or referring to 'she' instead of 'he'. Most men were called 'Lottie' or 'Clara'—and of course her favourite cognomen 'cunty'.

Members and regular guests were inured to the crude banter and homosexual innuendo, but new visitors were properly shocked by the lewd language. When long-standing member Daniel Farson, the erstwhile TV celebrity and chronicler of Soho, signed in John Braine, the Bradford-born author of the best-selling novel *Room at the Top*, Braine's seemingly pompous persona immediately invoked Belcher's critical tongue: 'She's not a pretty lady, is she?'

Members at the bar chortled at the put-down. Braine did not appreciate the gay comment and said so, Muriel responded by showing him the door, saying, 'On your way, Lottie, before I give you a fourpenny one!' The embarrassed author left the sinful place with laughter ringing in his ears. But he was not alone in suffering her insults. In particular, tight-fisted members were singled out and induced to 'Open your bead-bag, cunty, and buy some drinkettes!'

In its early years the club was rather smart and sophisticated, but as the decades passed it became neglected and threadbare, drink-sodden and faded, much like many of its surviving members. Muriel died in 1979 and Ian Board kept the place going. He could be more outrageous than Belcher. At closing time he would usually declare: 'My name's Ian fucking Board, and I'm bored stiff with the lot of you—so piss off!' Francis Bacon died in 1992 aged 82. Ian Board succumbed to lung cancer in 1994; he was 63 but looked ten years older. The club passed into the hands of Board's loyal barman Michael Wojas, who was mainly addicted to vodka. The Colony, a shadow of its former self, lingered on until Wojas, under pressure from his landlord to vacate, finally closed the moribund room in 2008. Wojas died of an alcohol-related illness in 2010.

I happened to be in the club when the BBC sent in a team to interview Wojas and film the end of a Soho legend for a TV *Newsnight* item. And through my connections within the BBC, I managed to obtain a disc of the film, an animated souvenir of a bunch of Colony veterans drinking at the bar for the last time. Derek and I were never paid-up members; we were always there as guests. He was not enamoured of the place. It was too overly gay for his liking. I found the members unusual and amusing and I often laughed at the high-flying expletives being lobbed back and forth in cultured, well-modulated voices. After its demise there was much talk of replicating the place, a new Colony for a new era. But it never happened. It remains unique in Soho history. It also remains unique in my personal history (and I also speak for Derek here)—at no other club or pub, past or present, have I ever been addressed as 'cunty'.

Francis Bacon was, and remains, one of the greatest of British painters of the 20th century. He also reaped immense monetary gain from his art, becoming a millionaire in his lifetime. Today, his paintings sell for multi-millions. Leaving aside the quality and artistic merit of his controversial work, the man himself was as complicated as his art. A flamboyant homosexual of the masochistic strain, he enjoyed and apparently thrived on ulta-violent sex. In other words, he took great pleasure in being brutalised and then buggered. His deviant sexuality was formed, it is claimed, by his appalling childhood. Born in Ireland in 1909 to a cruel and callous father, he was regularly whipped and sexually assaulted by savage and ignorant stable boys on his father's horse-breeding estate.

For partners in his bizarre sexual contract he preferred 'lovers' from the lower classes—'rough trade' as it is known in the homosexual demi-monde. The most notable of these companions being George Dyer, an uneducated East-End Cockney who spoke in the traditional 'fink' (think) and 'fort' (thought) manner. His strangulated speech pattern was further compounded by a slight impediment and his unconstrained use of raw expletives. Bacon, who spoke like an Edwardian toff, often mocked him.

'Francis, I fort that...' And Francis would intervene with a smug, 'Oh, yes, George, and whom did you fight?'

Dyer had a dismal upbringing. He had been to Borstal (a young offenders institution) and had served prison time. He led the life of a petty criminal before becoming Bacon's catamite, and had associated with the notorious Kray Twins, Reggie and Ronnie; mainly with Ronnie, whose gay activities were well known to the homosexual community.

George was a walking time-bomb, just waiting to explode. Withdrawn, cautious of strangers, and reserved when sober or after a few drinks, but when drunk or provoked he could be a thorough bastard, bang out of order. He had an air of menace about him, a hovering threat of violence. Bacon often appeared in his Soho haunts with a black eye, bruised face and cut lip, which he sported much like a heterosexual would display a female love-bite on his neck. They had met in a Soho pub in 1964, Dyer being some twenty years younger than Bacon, who was 55. The now wealthy artist gave his 'boy' lots of money to keep him happy.

In a dark Savile Row suit and discreet necktie George could pass as a successful businessman or banker. But when he opened his Cockney mouth in cultured company—disaster! From banker to wanker in very short order. During their relationship he became a liability and a nuisance. But Bacon adored him and they 'loved' each other in their own peculiar manner. Dyer also served his paymaster in the role of artistic muse. Bacon painted his naked, muscular torso numerous times. Dyer, himself, was never ever interested in art. Indeed, he disliked Bacon's 'Elephant-man' portraits: 'I fink they're 'orrible and I don't really understand wot they mean'.

George went beyond the pale when, in a fit of jealous vengeance, he informed the police that Francis smoked illegal drugs in the studio. The cops raided the place and arrested the artist. It was a vindictive and empty betrayal. The artist stood trial and was quickly acquitted. Bacon forgave him and they continued their turbulent 'love' affair until death finally parted them.

Derek and I first met George Dyer way back in the late 1940s at London's Feldman Club at 100 Oxford Street, the cradle of the infant bebop modern jazz movement newly arrived from the United States. We were fans of the new music and its American innovators. We were impressed by the sharp, slick appearance and attire of the bebop jazz stars such as the 'cool' black trumpeter Miles Davis, Lennie Tristano, piano, Lee Konitz, alto sax, Gil Evans, piano, Charlie Ventura, tenor sax, and the elegant black singer and bandleader, Billy Eckstine. Especially the latter who sported the much-coveted big, rolled-collar shirt.

But in those austerity-ridden, early post-war days Britain still had clothes rationing and stylish attire for teenagers was virtually impossible to obtain. 'Georgie' Dyer, as he was then called, helped fill the need. Always dressed in fashionable, American-style 'drape' suits or jackets, he served as the club's resident spiv who peddled genuine Yankee gear—shirts, ties, socks, baseball jackets—brought in by crew members of the transatlantic liners and merchant ships. The teenage Derek, as a merchant seaman, spent most of his pay on buying clothes in New York.

At this time of his life, he was about twenty, 'Georgie' was perceived to be heterosexual and proved successful with the girls, despite his youthful acne. He sold his imported merchandise and other gear from a small van, which was also fitted-out with a mattress to accommodate his female conquests. We envied his mobile bedroom. So when did his sexual proclivity change? Perhaps he was always bisexual and the 'homo' side prevailed in later years? Dyer the Dealer obtained a batch of Billy Eckstine-style shirts and quickly sold the lot. Derek and I were among the lucky few. Factory-folded, pinned, with a stiffener, the shirts looked the real thing... however, when unfolded for wear they revealed a fundamental flaw—they were all missing the right sleeve!

They were, of course, factory rejects repackaged. Dyer

refused to refund our money, claiming he had also been duped, and promised to punish the fraudster. We came to laugh at the experience and called the amputated shirts the 'Wingy Manone Special', after the one-armed American jazz trumpeter Joe 'Wingy' Manone. Manone lost his right arm in a streetcar accident at the age of ten. It is said that Joe Venuti, the jazz violinist and notorious prankster, used to send 'Wingy' a single cufflink every Christmas. Manone, was in fact, fitted with a prosthetic arm, which held up the trumpet, the only instrument that can be played, quite naturally, with one hand.

Some fifteen years after his Feldman Club days, George the 'nobody' met Francis the famous painter and so began his eventual self-destruction. The inadequate, unproductive Dyer couldn't cope with his new lifestyle and slowly drowned in the waterfall of wealth showered upon him by his millionaire lover. George, unpretentious and vernacular in his choice of Soho drinking companions, was acutely aware of his social and cultural limitations. He kept away from Bacon's intellectual friends. Francis, on the other hand, minced easily and with utter confidence through the clearly divided caste system of London society—from the dire drinking dens of Soho to grand salons and palaces. Where Dyer was tongued-tied at the 'top table' so to speak, Bacon the pompous polymath could voice an opinion on most subjects. So George withdrew from Bacon's other world and preferred the louche company of his loser mates who helped him spend Bacon's money. George was drinking and drugging himself into oblivion.

Their violent and now unhappy relationship came to a fatal conclusion in October 1972 when George reluctantly accompanied Bacon to Paris for the illustrious opening of the artist's retrospective exhibition at the Grand Palais. On the day Bacon attended a lavish state reception hosted by President Pompidou, the redundant Cockney muse died alone in their room at the Hotel St Peres after taking a massive overdose of drugs. Soon after the tragic event Bacon, in a mood of remorseful inspiration, painted his *Triptych-May-June 1973*: three panels, oil on canvas, depicting the awful demise of his lover. The *Triptych*, now in a private collection in Switzerland, was purchased at auction for more than £3 million. So in death, George the 'nobody' had become famous and immortal.

There is a final twist to the George Dyer story. In 1998, Francis and George were brought back to cinematic life in the feature film *Love Is the Devil* directed by John Maybury. Derek Jacobi is a remarkable physical reincarnation as Bacon, in facial likeness and extravagant mannerisms. Daniel Craig delivers a perfect impersonation of Dyer, all repressed anger and bemused despair. In 2006, Craig was presented to the world's cinema audiences as the new James Bond in *Casino Royale*. I wonder what George Dyer would have thought of that?

*****

Gerry's Club was founded and run for many years by the actor Gerald Campion, celebrated for playing the fat public schoolboy Billy Bunter in the 1950s TV series. First established in Shaftsbury Avenue, the club attracted actors across the theatrical spectrum. It then moved premises to Dean Street, Soho, near *The French* pub, where it was taken over by the soft-spoken but fearless Michael Dillon, who served behind the bar and kept the house in order with a firm but subtle hand, although he allowed Derek a long leash of tolerance.

Derek patronised the basement club frequently, especially after a late-night performance, when he needed to unwind among convivial company. The writer Ian Ratcliffe closely observed the volatile Derek and a thinly veiled character appears in Ratcliffe's unpublished *roman a clef* called *The Tenor of Soho* in which Derek is portrayed as Doric Newbold. I quote from the manuscript at some length:

> 'Right, who wants a fight?' bellowed Doric Newbold as he exploded into the Glengarry Club [*Gerry's*]. Some of the less frequent habitues recoiled in shock at this bristling man with his bollocking charisma. Jonathan Jarvis swivelled placidly towards him. He had seen this performance from Doric before, particularly if Doric had been on stage that evening. He would arrive at this late drinker pumped up with adrenalin and bursting for a vodka fix.
>
> He greeted Doric cautiously, as one would an ex-Coldstream Guardsman of some sixteen stones and aggressive mien. But he knew that... as often as not, he ended the night weeping like an alcoholic baby through nothing save insecurity and post-production depression. Jarvis liked him, though. Newbolt was not one of those self-absorbed Thespians who bored one rigid with their dubious past triumphs and their desperation to be loved. No, Doric was a proper bloke.

He played hard, got drunk and took the consequences, without a scintilla of self-delusion... Jarvis bought him a drink... 'Fuck the Lyceum [Theatre]' snorted Doric between swift mouthfuls. 'That fucking director made a bloody poncified speech about Sir bloody Henry Irving and I said fuck Henry Irving and fuck the Lyceum!'... Jarvis let him bang on, for he knew that the real cause of Doric's suffering was a self-inflicted split in his long-standing marriage.

Over his shoulder, Jarvis noted that Doric was becoming embroiled in a discussion with a dodgy pair, whom he had nicknamed the Smug Brothers... The volume from Doric's neck of the woods was steadily increasing. Jarvis was receiving him loud and clear: 'What's your fucking game, eh? South East Asia? You were never there. I bayoneted my way through the fucking jungle with three stripes and a crown up, and you try to tell me you've been a poncy foreign correspondent?' The faux journalist and his catamite were nervously edging away from the gathering monsoon...

Suddenly the erstwhile foreign correspondent cannoned across the room, blood spurting from his nose on to his mulberry waistcoat... 'You're a liar and a ponce. But worst of all, you're a monumental bore. Take that from a defender of Queen and Country,' declared Doric, fuming beneath his sectored cap... Newbolt eyeballed the assembled company: 'Right! Does anyone else want a fight?'—'Now, Doric, you're being naughty,' cautioned Marcus McDublin [Michael Dillon] 'That's quite enough for now. We're all going to our beds.'

Ratcliffe's passage captures Derek's speech and references perfectly—plus his sudden explosion into violence. Doric's allusion to the Lyceum signalled his final performance with the Cottesloe company, in the last segment of *The Mysteries,* which had transferred to the West End theatre. Because of financial difficulties Peter Hall closed down the Cottesloe stage space for some six months; the productions there had been heavily subsidised. Derek's contract with the NT concluded in April 1985 and was not renewed. It was the end of a ten-year tenure for Derek, a decade of varied and successful performances.

CHAPTER 13

'Do you want to fight me?'

Alcohol affects people in many different ways. It depends on one's own inner secret self. To some it helps liberate the creative mind. To some it eases the constraints of shyness. In others it acts as a soporific. It can also exacerbate an innate aggression and intolerance to any criticism, no matter how mild or justified. Derek's father drank deeply from the latter cup, and so did he. He could be laughing and amusing at one moment, then, a perceived word out of place, and he suddenly became a baneful drunk. But he never saw himself as a boring boozer or bullying drunkard. He viewed himself simply as a 'drinker'—as if it were a recognised profession.

'You're not a drinker, Peter,' he would say to me, 'you don't understand.'

I am not an abstemious person. I enjoy a drink, or two, or more. I drink wine with dinner. I drink brandy with a good cigar. I am, in my humble opinion, a decent social drinker. I have learned the hard way to realise when I've had enough. Alcoholics have no such boundary: they drink—like Derek—until they are bang-out-of-order. They drink themselves to an early grave. Derek referred to his chronic condition as a disease, a sickness he could not control. I called it an addiction, self-inflicted, that could be cured through self-discipline. Of course, he rejected and resented my simplistic diagnosis. We argued bitterly over the subject. I still believe that his deep-rooted reason for imbibing so heavily was a desire to behave badly—and to blame his bad behaviour on the alcohol.

I once had the temerity to suggest that he might seek help from Alcoholics Anonymous. He responded sharply with: 'Why should I submit myself to a bunch of losers spilling out my guts... I don't need the fucking AA... and I don't need your chicken-shit advice!' And that was the end of that. He did however at the persistence of his much-concerned wife, make several attempts to kick the habit, to get on the water-wagon. But each essay proved to be a short-lived experiment during which time he became a boring, smug, acrimonious pain-up-the-anus; a man on the outside desperately trying to stay sober, but his inner-demon dying for a drink.

It came as quite a shock to me when—at a gathering of family and friends shortly after Derek's death—his eldest son Quentin informed me that Derek had claimed that I was the cause of his alcoholism! How on earth was it my fault? It was a ridiculous statement and I laughed at the bizarre accusation. But then Derek himself had said that he had inherited the drinking gene (or 'genie') from his father. And another time he blamed his faithful and long-suffering wife Jean for his dreadful addiction. Everybody, it seems, was to blame but himself. No *mea culpa*. It was, of course, the classic alcoholic's excuse.

During Derek's first period of abstinence, my wife and I were invited to a weekend stay at his Purley home. We sat in the living room waiting for our usual pre-dinner drink. Derek, newly sober, energetic, was buzzing around like a blue-arse fly: in the kitchen one moment stirring a pot, then laying the dining-room table. Seemingly, the model husband and host. Then Jean called out to him, 'Have you given them a drink, yet?' And the now abstemious Derek reacted slowly as if the request was an unimportant item, 'Oh, yes, of course... I forgot.'

A little later, with a steady, oh-so-temperate hand he dispensed our 'necessary poison.' I said to him mockingly, 'Thank God, Derek, we thought you'd never ask.' His eyes flickered for a hostile instant, then he buzzed off again while we sipped in pleasure.

Later in the evening, while we enjoyed a few more drinks and made light-hearted family conversation, the Puritan-like Derek sat upright on the edge of his chair, watching and waiting like a bird of prey. His critical eyes and ears keenly alert to the slightest half-baked statement or jovial comment we might make in our cups. He would then swoop to reprove his victim and deliver his sober and sensible opinion. He was not joyful company. No drink, no humour. Abstinence changed his persona radically from his former convivial, amusing self— to a hypercritical, sanctimonious, pompous bore. Paradoxically, I much preferred Derek the drinker. However, his brave attempts at sobriety did not last long, a couple of weeks maybe, six months at the longest.

It was clear to me that his high intake of alcohol was affecting his hitherto amiable personality, his social outlook. His charm was decreasing and his cynicism growing. He could no longer engage in small talk, or to be pleasant, with people he considered not worthy of his attention, that is, people who could not further his career. But he would flatter and cultivate those who could. He was, in fact, turning into a textbook theatrical opportunist. He was also becoming blatantly self-obsessed. Marlon Brando once said: 'An actor's a guy who, if you ain't talking about him, he ain't listening.' Derek was becoming that actor. Off-stage, alcohol was beginning to affect his social conversation. He became lax in his speaking manner, peppering his racy anecdotes with slang words and raw expletives. Sometimes it was funny, other times offensive.

It was, I believe, Derek's constant use of the vulgar slang term 'wanker' that popularised the epithet at the Royal Court Theatre and later at the Cottesloe and the National Theatre. It was used as a dismissive insult against all in the acting profession outside the close-knit communities of the above theatres. Quite apart from its original sexual meaning, a 'wanker' meant a theatre person who spoke or behaved in a pretentious, silly or showy manner. As opposed to the serious, socially minded, kitchen-sink productions so admired by Derek's tribe of earnest thespians always 'striving for the truth'. Derek also made popular the slang expression 'bottle'—as in 'You've lost yer bottle!'—when reproving a fellow actor for under-performing: it meant the person so accused had lost his cutting edge, lost his nerve, his boldness. Conversely it could be used in praise: 'He's got bottle... good man!' The origin of this slang word is difficult to define. But Derek certainly made it common currency among the London theatrical community.

Deep in drink Derek was unpredictable. He could explode like a volcano. He even turned violently on me, his loyal and

BANG OUT OF ORDER!

tolerant brother. I was not a rival in his career, rather a sibling rival on the road to commercial success. But I was not a threat in any normal way. In fact, we were writing a boxing drama together (well, I was mostly doing the creative writing, he doing the talking and acting out various scenes) that we hoped to place with a TV company. We created a rollicking costume series set in Regency England featuring the rise of bare-knuckle prize-fighter named *Jem Starr*. And of course it contained a key, standout supporting role for Derek, as the scowling villainous ring rival of the young hero. Jon Pertwee was interested in a leading part.

At this time, 1986, I was establishing myself in the publishing business. I was happily married with a son newly-graduated from university. I mention these personal details because I believe Derek was jealous, and resented my growing prosperity, my stable marital status, and my moderate drinking. Our elder brother George was also doing well in business. It seemed evident to me that in Derek's egotistical mindset, that for him to succeed in life, his brothers must fail, and to be seen to fail. But it did not happen that way.

About the violent episode. I had arranged to meet Derek for lunch at *Kettner's* in Soho, my treat. I sat at the restaurant table and waited. He was late, as usual. At first he was convivial, talking about the progress of the *Jem Starr* story. Gradually things turned sour. We had two bottles of wine during the meal. I noticed that, although we seemed to be drinking the same amount, he was decidedly getting more inebriated than I was. At frequent intervals he would go to the toilet. In comparison, I went only once during the entire lunch. I suddenly realised, and later confirmed, that instead of taking a pee, he was swigging covert shots of vodka from a half bottle, a flat bottle he had hidden in his inside jacket pocket. His attitude toward me was slowly becoming hostile.

From *Kettner's,* we went to the *Kismet Club*, where he had arranged to meet his girlfriend Elizabeth. Derek was now openly downing vodka, no need to be furtive about it. He was well boozed. Loud-mouthed and insulting. He said something nasty to Lizzie that upset her and, drama-queen that she was, tears started to well up.

'Why can't you be a gentleman, like Peter?' she said to Derek.

That did it. That lit the waiting fuse.

'Peter, a gentleman...You must be kidding! Peter, a fucking gentleman. What a laugh...'

A bad scene was developing and I tried to circumvent it.

'Derek, can I have a word outside.'

We walked into the narrow passageway.

'You shouldn't talk to Elizabeth like that,' I said. 'And why are you insulting me?'

In reply, he promptly pushed me roughly against the wall and pressed his red, angry face close to mine. His vodka breath was nauseous.

'Don't ever, ever tell me what to say and do... you sanctimonious cunt! Shove your prissy advice up your self-righteous arsehole. I don't need you... now fuck-off and leave me alone.'

This verbal outburst left me utterly lost for words. I could see in his blazing eyes that, in this moment of madness, he actually wanted to smash his fist into my 'interfering' face. Thank the Lord that he managed to restrain himself. He released his grip and I walked out into the street in a shaking daze. It was the first and only time that he had laid hands on me and spoke with such anger.

On the way home, I kept going over the awful incident again and again. His sudden transformation into a raging monster baffled and scared me. A few days later he rang me as if nothing had happened.

'Peter, Bill Bryden is interested in *Jem Starr*. Can you send him a copy of the script so far?'

I was amazed at his now calm and composed manner. He had indeed become a real-life *Dr Jekyll and Mr Hyde* character; transformed from his normal self by excessive drinking, compounded perhaps, by domestic stress and career frustration. I was in no mood for sibling reconciliation. I was still smarting from his previous cruel and unjustified outburst.

'I don't give a damn about Bill Bryden,' I snapped. 'And I don't give a damn about you or *Jem Starr*. Don't call me again.' I slammed the phone down.

We did not speak again for about a year. Alas, *Jem Starr* never entered the roped square. The project, promising though it was, was over as far as I was concerned. I could never work with Derek again. And he did not possess the writing ability, nor the writing focus necessary, nor the solitary discipline to go it alone. He was an ensemble player, a team member who needed company in which to function.

During our period of mutual silence, Elizabeth his girlfriend kept me informed by phone of Derek's ill-fated antics, his *Rake's Progress* if you will. She told me about the drunken Durkin incident. Patrick 'Paddy' Durkin was a burly, curly-haired actor with the mug of a prize-fighter; a small-part player of stage and screen, usually cast as a TV baddy or bodyguard. He was also a former straight man to comedian magician Tommy Cooper. Derek and Paddy were close drinking mates. I never took to the man. He annoyed me from the very start by always greeting, and addressing me as 'Mrs' Newark. He also called Derek 'Mrs' Newark. He wasn't homosexual. It was just an irritating and continuous 'camp' theatrical affectation that he considered amusing. It soon ceased to be funny to me, just tedious and irksome.

When Durkin's doctor advised him to stop drinking or he would soon die, he managed to kick the alcohol and he opened a small hotel or restaurant. He invited his old friend Derek, and Lizzie, to a party at the place and they dressed-up for the occasion: she in glamorous frock, he in white tuxedo and black tie. 'We looked a million dollars,' she said. As the boozy evening progressed, the steadily imbibing Derek inevitably became abusive and bellicose towards the other guests, and to his now sober host. Durkin tried his best to calm down and control his former drinking pal, but to no avail.

Derek, the uncontrollable, continued to upset the party until the exasperated Durkin, with the help of another brawny chap, had to physically constrain and remove the inebriated Derek and the distressed Elizabeth from the premises—in short, they threw him out, still ranting. The white tuxedo now stained and ripped and the relationship with Durkin well and truly over.

BANG OUT OF ORDER!

Another outrageous performance brought to a shabby ending. Patrick Durkin died in 2009, still sober at 73, so I am told.

Elizabeth also told me about the notorious 'Spanish incident'. Derek got a job filming for a TV commercial in a Spanish resort and took Lizzie along for the jaunt. He drank steadily on the plane and at the hotel, despite his own professional resolution, his actor's credo, his oft-repeated mantra that, 'Drink as much as you like, but drink should never, ever compromise or interfere with one's theatrical performance... business is paramount... one should never let the team down.' Despite all that ingrained conviction and belief, Derek drank himself into such a state of inebriation that he could not complete his engagement. One night he suffered a severe case of delirium tremens (the dreaded DTs) and imagined all kinds of bugs and creatures crawling over him. In blind terror he ran out of the hotel virtually naked and was brought back like a lunatic by the Spanish police. He and Lizzie were put on a plane accompanied by a white-coated male nurse on the TV company's payroll. A sad, shameful episode that damaged his reputation.

Jean Thornhill had married Derek in April 1958. She was several years older than he. In the early period of their marriage they were a happy, ambitious couple with a young family and a large suburban house; Derek a good father and contented husband. But after nearly 30 stormy years together, the loyal and long-suffering Jean could no longer endure his womanising and the humiliation, his increasing alcohol consumption, and his constant verbal and physical abuse. Once, when she mentioned the subject of divorce, he threatened to 'Burn the fucking house down!' Jean was granted a *decree nisi* in November 1987 and a *decree absolute* in February 1988.

Following his divorce from Jean and selling the family home at Purley, Derek and his current lover the fiery, flirtatious Elizabeth, moved into a basement flat at Primrose Hill, near Regents Park, paying £120 weekly. It was here during a drunken argument that Derek knocked Lizzie through a glazed door and she called the police, whom Derek treated with sneering contempt. Fortunately, she suffered only minor injuries and refused to press charges.

Told to vacate the flat, they moved to a cheaper one in Fulham at £95 weekly. Money was getting tight but Derek always relied on another feature film payment to save the day. And it did. He got second billing to Bernard Hill in the crime movie *Bellman and True* in which he played a vicious gang leader. This enabled him, in October 1988, to purchase a decent flat via a hefty mortgage at Barons Keep, a large private residential complex near Barons Court tube station. It would be his final abode. His 10 years there would prove tempestuous, coping with the moody Elizabeth, and after her departure, the unstable Shabnam.

Drugs played little or no part in Derek's downfall. Vodka and brandy floated his boat into the Lake of the Lost. As impressionable teenagers, we both flirted with smoking marijuana, being keen enthusiasts of the London jazz club scene, where 'Mary Warner', as it was dubbed, was freely available among the modern bebop-playing musicians that we admired. In truth, the dried leaves and flower clusters of the hemp plant had pigmy effect on our senses. We laughed uncontrollably and acted silly because that was the expected result of smoking a 'joint'. But it was mostly a deed of self-delusion—it was 'hip' to be seen to be 'high'.

I suspect that Derek indulged in smoking some kind of hemp plant while serving as a soldier in the Far East. I remember standing in the green-house of his home in Purley when he pointed to several potted plants placed under some lights, saying, 'Pot!' with some emphasis.

'Yes,' I replied, 'nice pots.'

'No, no... it's pot! Cannabis,' and he laughed at my show of surprise.

When I went to New York to see him in *Bedroom Farce* in 1979, he was smoking marijuana then. He rolled me a joint and gave me a chocolate bar to chew with the smoke, advising me that it enhanced the euphoric effect. But I found the combination did little to heighten any sense of narcotic nirvana. I was not seduced by Mary Warner and remained loyal to old Jack Daniels. As far as I knew, Derek never indulged in cocaine or heroin or other hard drugs, although his lover the madcap Elizabeth did sniff the white stuff.

*****

At the beginning of 1991, Derek's career was at a very low ebb. He had no work and no income. Lizzie left him, saying she was bored with living with a drunken old has-been always banging on about past glories. He was well rid of her but it didn't boost his ego. His professional reputation had been badly damaged by the Hochhuth stage fiasco, and he was under threat of eviction from Barons Keep for non-payment of service charges. And to compound the utter misery of this sorry state, he crashed over in his flat and 'broke' his neck! If not actually broken it was severely injured.

He maintained that he was not drunk at the time but tripped over a rug. In hospital, he was fitted with a metal frame clamped to his head and shoulders to support his fragile neck. When I made the feeble jest about rehearsing for *The Man in the Iron Mask* he was not amused. Apparently his behaviour in hospital was out of order and they discharged him earlier than expected. They were glad to see the back of him.

As a *bona fide* actor-invalid, unemployed and without visible means, he was advised to apply for financial relief from the established show business charities. In July 1991, he approached the Actors Benevolent Fund (ABF) and the Royal Theatrical Fund (RTF). Both applications were successful. The ABF allotted him a modest £10 per week over a long period. The RTF committee granted him a substantial one-off payment to tide him over, and another similar award in 1992. Somehow he managed to hold on to his flat at Barons Keep. His neck healed and the 'iron mask' came off. The screws that had held the frame in position now left two deep indentations on his forehead, one either side, as if a pair of devil horns had been shorn off! He made fun of his new appearance: 'The only part I'm fit for is a man with two holes in his head.'

At this sorry point in his flagging career, Derek decided to take himself into the wilderness—that is, he went to work 'up North'. He got some BBC radio projects in Birmingham, and toured the Northern circuit with a low-budget 'chicken-feed' production, as he described it. During this period of theatrical purdah, the writer Keith Waterhouse, who knew Derek from way back, paid him a visit in some small-town theatre where he was sharing a dressing room with two unknown young actors. Derek was harping on about his dire current situation, the poor quality of the show and so on.

'What the fuck am I doing here? I'm better than this... I'm a West End actor... but those fat bastards won't give me another chance...'

Just then, one of those 'bastards'—a prominent London impresario—walked in to be greeted by Derek's angry welcome.

'And you can piss-off... you blood-sucking ponce!'

Little wonder that Derek was not in favour by the movers and shakers of show business. It was during this period of northern exile that he met Shabnam, a Pakistani girl of modern outlook from an orthodox family. She had dreams of becoming a singer and Derek spun her family the line that he would like to take her to London—the city of opportunity—and he would guide and look after her. He would be her mentor with no hanky-panky involved! She could stay in the spare bedroom at his flat and they could visit any time. The family agreed and that was the beginning of their relationship.

Sadly, she turned out to be another lame duck like Elizabeth, although it must be said, Derek was well nigh impossible to live with. The flat at Barons Keep was a troubled place. Shabnam soon developed into a domestic problem. The disingenuous promise he had made to her family regarding a platonic relationship had long been thrown out of the high window of Barons Keep. It had, of course, quickly developed into a consensual sexual coupling. According to Derek's diagnosis, Shabnam was somewhat mentally unstable. After a fierce altercation concerning her untidy habits and ungrateful attitude and other irritating factors, he told her to leave for good and she went.

'Where's she gone to?' I asked over the phone.

'I don't know and I don't care. Back to poxy Bradford I suppose. She's not my problem anymore.'

But Shabnam had not entirely made her exit from this complicated scene. Derek told me that he had received news that she had been sectioned under the Mental Health Act and committed to a 'loony bin', as he so delicately put it. Feeling guilty he went to see her, and she told him in no uncertain manner to 'fuck off!' A month later Derek called me with the scary news that Shabnam had left the hospital and had phoned him to say that she intended to come to his flat and knife him— and would he pay the taxi fare? I laughed at this seriocomic turn of events. But Derek was not in a jovial mood. He called the police and was advised not to open the door and to phone 999 at the first sign of trouble. I did not know what to make of this farcical situation. He eventually took her back and she remained at Barons Keep to the very end of his life.

One afternoon in the early 1990s, Derek and I sat drinking in the *Kismet Club*. I can't remember the exact date but I clearly recall what transpired that day. Derek was in a belligerent mood. Every actor he knew in the place being, in his considered opinion, a 'cunt'. The *Kismet* was a basement drinking dive in Little Newport Street, opposite The Arts Theatre. It opened at three in the afternoon and catered for a cross-section of regulars: jobbing thespians, writers, fringe villains, homos and has-beens, and, of course, alcoholics. It was not in any way a sophisticated rendezvous but it had a seedy attraction, much like the seamy *Colony Room* in Dean Street, Soho.

At one time the *Kismet* was run by a tough ex-policeman who on one pugnacious occasion secured Derek in a headlock to prevent a punch-up. It seemed to me that the jukebox was always playing Dean Martin singing *Little Ole Wine Drinker Me*. Keith Waterhouse was fond of telling the story of the newcomer to the dive who asked, 'What's that strange smell?' And the veteran actor and drinker Freddie Jones replied, 'Desperation, old boy, desperation'. Because it attracted the theatrical crowd, the *Kismet* was also known as the 'Den of Equity'.

As I have mentioned, Derek was in an ugly mood. His career was at a standstill. And he was surrounded by 'cunts'. He was in his 'Do you want to fight me?' mode. This bullying challenge worked on the presumption that most people do not wish to settle an argument, or difference of opinion, with fisticuffs. So, if like Derek, you were big and heavy, loud and aggressive, the tactic was quite effective. 'Do you want to fight me?' usually resulted in the other guy submitting to the threat of superior force, uttering something conciliatory and moving away—generally accompanied by Derek's boastful gibe, 'That's right, sunshine, off you go!' I witnessed the scene a few times and I didn't like it

We left the *Kismet* and walked along Charing Cross Road to a pub, the name of which I can't remember. Ray Winstone, the up-and-coming Cockney hard man actor, was standing at the bar with a group of mixed gender company, one of whom was a black girl. Derek and Winstone knew each other and immediately fell into conversation and exchanged banter.

BANG OUT OF ORDER!

Some drinks later the congeniality suddenly turned sour when Derek said something that clearly upset the black girl. What he said I don't know as I was talking to someone else at the time. Winstone instantly came to the girl's defence.

'That's enough, Derek, you're out of order.'

Derek did not like to be reproved. '

I'm out of order!' he replied, his voice getting louder.

'Yeah, bang out of order... you should apologize,' countered Winstone, calmly.

Derek, his anger rising, glared at Winstone, almost nose to nose. Both were six feet tall and brawny.

'Out of order, am I? said Derek. Then came the old reliable challenge. 'Do you want to fight me? Then come outside.'

This time it was a big mistake. He had picked on the wrong man.

Winstone stared back, rock-hard and resolute, and said softly with the cocky confidence of a fighter: 'Derek, if I come outside I'll kill you.'

They continued to glower at each other until my brother, the first to blink, turned abruptly away from the confrontation and, without another word, stormed out. Derek was not a coward. Yes, he got his comeuppance. But he was right to walk away from such an uneven contest. Winstone looked fit, was in his thirties, and was ready to rumble. Derek was more than 20 years older and in very poor condition. He could sense, as I certainly did, the real danger in Ray's determined and fearless stance.

What we did not know at the time was that Winstone had been a champion amateur boxer as a teenager, had engaged in some 80 bouts and had represented England. Had it come to fisticuffs, he would indeed have inflicted serious damage on Derek. After he left the emotional scene, I mumbled some feeble, placatory nonsense to the stony-faced Winstone, the 'winner'. There was nothing I could say or do to alleviate the tense situation, and I scuttled out in Derek's wake.

I found him in the *Kismet*, sitting silent and chastened, with his usual vodka and tonic. He showed no sign of shame, only a sour-faced sense of being bested. Without saying a word he seemed to acknowledge the folly of his performance. I chose not to hold a post mortem on the ill-staged pub sequence, and he did not say another word about it. The show was over and done with. We never spoke about the incident again. And never again did I hear him issue the challenge, 'Do you want to fight me?'

To give him credit, Derek at sixty, was still full of fighting spirit. Some six months after the Winstone affair he related another confrontation that he had recently experienced. He was walking from a high street store carrying a frozen chicken in a plastic bag, when three rowdy youths barged past him on the pavement, nearly knocking him over. He gave them a mouthful of expletives that stopped them in their tracks. They turned and one of them, presumably the leader of the pack, swaggered up to Derek and said, 'What did you call me? You old git!'

That did it.

Derek said 'Cop for this!'

And he swung the solid bag, sending the youth flying. The three of them ran off like rabbits.

'It's a good thing I'm not vegetarian,' Derek said to me. 'A bag of green stuff wouldn't have been as effective as the frozen chicken I was carrying.'

In a mood of despondency in 1994, at the age of 61, financial desperation drove Derek to apply for a mundane job in the catering industry. He filled in an application for the position of Section Manager with Forte Restaurants, 'Anywhere in the London area', with a salary expectation of £250 weekly. He was somewhat disingenuous in ticking the question boxes. He stated his education, his Merchant Navy service, his five-year Army record, his RADA and theatre experience. In answer to the question 'What have been the most important events or people in your own development and Why?' Derek wrote:

> I worked with William Bryden OBE and Sir Peter Hall whilst spending eleven years at the National Theatre. Both taught me an immense about Theatre, Drama, and man management.

Having completed the application, Derek must have had a change of mind. In the signature space at the end of the form Derek wrote—'A silly old cunt!' And shoved the document in his desk drawer and forgot about it. I discovered it many years later when going through his papers. Anyway, thank you Derek for a last posthumous laugh.

Throughout his last few years, Derek was deep in debt and degradation and still drinking heavily, with enforced bouts of sobriety. In May 1995, he was rushed to hospital having consumed two bottles of vodka in a single day. When he overcame this serious setback he tried desperately to cut down on the booze, taking Valium prescribed by a doctor. In November, he told me over the phone, he had cut down his consumption to half a bottle a day, and a few months later he had reduced this to ¼ bottle of vodka a day. So for his chronic condition he was virtually sober. His hard-working agent got him some work in *The Bill*, a popular police series by Thames Television, and he did several episodes. While there, he struck an almost immediate rapport with Kevin Lloyd, star of the show, who unfortunately was also a chronic alcoholic. And Derek began drinking again in his company.

In July 1996, he told me he owed the Inland Revenue £1,112, plus other debts. I took him to lunch at the *Ivy* in the vain hope of cheering him up. He was recovering from a four-day bender. My diary records: 'Derek in v bad way... looked awful, eyes red & running... terribly boring, kept repeating himself... v tiresome lunch. Saw him off in taxi.'

And yet he always seemed to recover from these serious setbacks. When I phoned a week later, he sounded quite normal and had managed to get a part-time job lecturing at the Actors' Studio. He was however beset by financial and domestic problems and seriously considered selling the Barons Keep flat because of its high service charges and began looking for a small, cheaper, one-bedroom apartment. He found a potential buyer for the flat at £87,000 but the transaction entailed paying off a £16,000 mortgage. He failed to find suitable other accommodation and the deal, compounded by further difficulties, fell through and the whole idea was abandoned, owing solicitors £475.

In September 1996, his financial situation was desperate: the £600 fee for *The Bill* had quickly been consumed by debt. He was committed to pay £50 per month to the implacable

Inland Revenue, £50 per month to Lloyds Bank, and £20 per month to the Department of Social Securities (DSS) for some over-payment error. All this to be paid out of £100 per week Income Support, and what little regular help from the Actors Benevolent Fund!

Then a grenade was tossed into his vulnerable financial trench—the DSS stopped payment because he had not registered on time, or something like that, most likely caused by his drunken state and failing memory. He appealed and was assured that he would be re-instated on 5 November. In the meantime he had nothing to live on, to buy food and other essentials. I immediately sent him some cash by post, which he deemed to be a 'debt of honour'. Nevertheless, there was a light at the end of the dark tunnel. A promised residual payment of some £30,000 world royalties due for his part in the TV mini-series *War and Remembrance* first shown in 1987. This life saving 'thirty grand' took on mythical proportions. His 'debt of honour' would be paid in full: 'When my boat comes in, Peter, when my boat comes in.' But it never did in his lifetime.

When next I saw him face to face he was in very bad shape. An old wreck of a man. He was 63 and looked 10 years older. He mumbled a lot and his dress appearance lacked attention. He walked with a stick to support his unreliable right leg. His ego had taken a terrible battering over his latter years. He confessed to me a final humiliation. His agent fixed an audition with a lady producer who knew his work from before. He smartened himself up and presented himself at the office reception area. The dozy young girl behind the desk buzzed the producer and said, quite loudly, to Derek's mortification:

'There's an old man here sez he's got an appointment... sez his name's Newmark... Derrin Newmark.'

When the producer appeared on the scene to clarify the situation she made a fuss of the 'old man'—'Derek! How lovely to see you...'

But the damage to his fragile self-esteem had been done. Gone were the days when his well-known TV face ensured instant recognition. He was very upset by the incident and it undermined his latest effort to control his intake of alcohol.

His outrageous consumption of vodka robbed him of at least a further 20 years of productive activity in the acting profession. Derek hated the inevitable process of growing old, far more, perhaps, than most people. To him, good looks and appearance were essential factors in his theatrical masquerade. At the age of 63, he disliked what he saw in the mirror. His once robust physique had turned to fat. His jaw line had developed a double-chin; his image reflected a bloated, blotched and bleary-eyed, sick and ageing alcoholic has-been. Gone was the athlete who once could perform a stunt or two. The upright Guardsman had long deserted. Both knees were now *hors de combat*; he could only walk with crutches. To borrow from the prose of Graham Greene, he was a 'burnt-out case' living on state benefits and charity. The final curtain was about to be lowered.

CHAPTER 14
The Final Curtain

Death by alcohol poisoning came early to particular drinking chums in the Green Room. Mark McManus was the first to leave prematurely. He and Derek became firm friends during the heady Cottesloe years. Both enjoyed rugby and boxing, and both were hard drinkers. After leaving the National, McManus was cast in the role that defined him for the rest of his short career. He starred in the highly successful TV crime series *Taggart* (1983-1994), in which he played the Glaswegian hard-nut police officer DCI Jim Taggart. Alas, Mark continued to imbibe heavily and, after several years of declining health, he died of alcohol-related illness: pneumonia brought on by liver failure, in June 1994 aged 59. Derek made the sad journey to his funeral in Glasgow. It's interesting to note that in 1975 Mark played, brilliantly, another ill-fated Glasgow hero, the world champion flyweight boxer Benny Lynch, in a play written by Bill Bryden. Lynch also fell victim to alcoholism and ended his days begging for drinks. He died in the gutter in 1946 aged only 33.

Robert Stephens was next to take the final exit. He died in November 1995 aged 64. A leading player in the infant years of the National Theatre he was, at one time, regarded as the natural successor to Sir Laurence Olivier. He starred in many films, including *The Prime of Miss Jean Brodie* (1969) with his then wife Maggie Smith, and played the title role in *The Private Life of Sherlock Holmes* in 1970. Following his departure from the NT and the break up of his marriage to Maggie Smith in 1973, he suffered a career slump, not helped by heavy smoking and excessive drinking and a nervous breakdown. He returned to the NT and appeared in several productions by the Cottesloe Company in the 1980s, one of which was the ill-conceived and badly-received pantomime *Cinderella* directed by Bill Bryden that featured Robert and Derek in outrageous 'drag' as the unfunny 'Ugly Sisters'.

Derek enjoyed Robert's bibulous and bitchy company at the Green Room bar where, vodka in hand, they would exchange irreverent anecdotes and critical comments about fellow thespians, their affectations and acting quirks and tricks. Stephens in particular disliked Laurence Harvey, the film star with the matinee-idol profile.

'That man,' he told Derek, 'was a really appalling human-being. And what's even more unforgivable... he was an appalling actor!'

It was Stephens, in his scabrous memoirs, *Knight Errant*, published in 1995, who first told the story of Laurence Olivier's explosive outrage at Harvey's unwarranted criticism of legendary actors Ralph Richardson, John Gielgud, and Paul Scofield. It happened at a dinner party. Olivier listened quietly to Harvey's outrageous diatribe and then exploded like a bomb.

'How dare you!' he screamed at the top of his voice. 'Call yourself an actor? You're not even a bad actor. You can't act at all, you fucking stupid hopeless snivelling cunt-faced cunty fucking shit-faced arse-hole...'

'God, it was awful,' recalled Stephens, 'Harvey was just flattened like a bug against the wall.'

It was Stephens who told Derek (and Derek passed on to me) the anecdote concerning Olivier when he was Director of the NT at the Old Vic. Larry, as Stephens always called him, was interviewing a keen young actor who wanted to join the company. Having probed the man's background, the great Sir Laurence decided to test the young thespian's mettle.

'Insult me!' he suddenly snapped.

'What...?' mumbled the surprised aspirant.

'Insult me—go on— insult me!'

The young man gulped and recovered his wits.

'But, sir, how on earth can I do that? You're my hero, my role model. I respect you too much. How can I possibly insult such a pompous, pretentious, self-important old CUNT like you!'

Needless to say, he got the part.

Stephens re-established himself at the top of his profession when the Royal Shakespeare Company invited him to play Falstaff in *Henry IV* in 1991, and in several other prestigious roles. He received the Laurence Olivier Theatre Award in 1993 as best Actor for his performance as Falstaff. He was knighted early in 1995. When he was in hospital mortally ill, Derek went to see him.

'He looked like death warmed up. His once handsome face emaciated. The first thing he said to me was "Hello, old boy... would you be kind enough to pop out and get me some fags?"'

He died in November 1995 aged 64 from complications during surgery. He had in fact succumbed to years of constant smoking and alcohol abuse. He was married four times and had two sons, Toby Stephens and Chris Larkin, both of whom became actors.

'It was very sad to see him go like that,' said Derek. 'I do miss his company. He was a great player and drinker.'

The Grim Reaper of show business was busy in the 1990s. In May 1996, Jon Pertwee died of a heart attack at the decent age of 76. Pertwee and Derek were old chums from the *Doctor Who* series of 1970-74 in which Derek had played the character Greg Sutton to Pertwee's popular Doctor Who.

Derek lost another drinking pal in March 1997 with the death of Ronald Fraser aged 66. A familiar supporting player in many films and TV series, his rotund figure, moon face, and fruity voice were instantly recognisable. He had great success in the TV series *The Misfit*, first broadcast in 1970, in which he was perfectly cast as the social misfit Badger, a hard-drinking ex-colonial tea-planter who found, on his return to England, that the old country had changed radically in his absence, and not to his liking. Fraser's favourite tipple was a large vodka with a dash of lime and soda, known to his drinking cronies as 'Fraser-water' and it achieved national fame as Badger's favourite drink.

August 1997 saw the demise of Bill Mitchell, a Canadian-born actor who became a local legend in London's Soho, where he lived and drank in the pubs and afternoon drinking clubs. A big bear-like figure always dressed in black, sporting a wide-brimmed black hat and dark glasses, he spoke slowly in a bass voice that earned him a lucrative living as a popular voice-over for commercial products, such as male aftershave, Pan

American airlines, and various brands of lager. When Orson Welles died in 1985, Mitchell took over his Carlsberg Lager voice-over role and was so convincing at imitating the famous film star's unique intonation that the general public couldn't tell the difference.

Once in the *French* pub in Dean Street, Derek got into an altercation with Mitchell and they agreed to go outside and settle the matter physically. Both fancied themselves as exponents of unarmed combat; Derek in judo, Mitchell in karate. They shaped up to each other with various dramatic kung fu gestures and postures... and then, realising how ludicrous they both looked, they burst out laughing and returned to the pub for another drink. Mitchell described himself as a 'professional drunk'. He was not an ambitious, competitive man. He viewed life as 'a concert not a contest'. He died at the age of 62 from too much smoking (to maintain his dark brown voice) and too much heavy drinking.

Brian Glover, a close colleague of Derek in the Cottesloe Company of the NT died in July 1997, aged 63. Although a regular and enthusiastic member of Bill Bryden's Green Room 'Rugby Team', Glover did not die of alcohol abuse but from a brain tumour. His simple gravestone bears the inscription 'Wrestler, Actor, Writer'. He was also a schoolteacher from 1954 to 1970. His father was a wrestler known as the 'Red Devil' and Brian campaigned in the sport under the ring name 'Leon Arras the Man from Paris', before becoming a film, TV and stage actor. His shaven head, stocky build, and gruff Yorkshire accent gained him many roles as tough guys and criminals.

Glover made an instant impact in his first acting role when he portrayed Mr Sugden, the comically overbearing sports teacher in Ken Loach's 1969 film *Kes*, a story about a boy's relationship with a baby kestrel. During his varied acting career on stage and television he played a number of Shakespearean roles—but always in his distinctive, unadulterated, native Yorkshire accent. His was the familiar Northern voice-over as the Tetley Tea man of the 1970s TV commercials, and for Allison's bread, all goodness 'Wi' nowt tekken out'.

With the coming year of 1998, Derek, himself suffering fragile health, experienced the untimely deaths of several more friends and colleagues. Daniel Massey, film star son of film star father Raymond Massey, was born in London in 1933, the same year as Derek. They first met when both were learning their trade in the Royal Shakespeare Company in May 1962. In November that year Derek and Daniel were flashing their blades and their teeth in Dumas's *The Three Musketeers* for a short season at The Nottingham Playhouse: Derek as Porthos and Daniel as Athos. The two musketeers became life-long friends. They next worked together in the 1970 film *Fragment of Fear*.

Daniel died of Hodgkin's lymphoma in March 1998, aged 64. Derek was much affected by his old friend's demise. When I phoned him, he kept repeating, 'Poor Daniel... poor Daniel... how very sad.' Derek was soon to join him in that crowded Green Room in the sky. Daniel Massey made his film debut at the tender age of nine when he played the son of ship's captain Noel Coward—his real-life godfather—in the 1942 propaganda film *In Which We Serve*. Some 25 years later, Daniel portrayed Coward in the movie *Star!* opposite Julie Andrews as Gertrude Lawrence, for which performance he won a Golden Globe Award.

The next colleague to drop permanently off the 'bar stool' was Kevin Lloyd, star of the popular TV police series, *The Bill*. In 1993, Derek, then aged 60, was undergoing a desperate bout of voluntary sobriety and his loyal, hardworking agent managed to get him into the cast of *The Bill*, produced by Thames Television, and he completed several episodes. While in the show, he struck an almost immediate affinity with Kevin Lloyd, who played the key role of Detective Constable Alfred 'Tosh' Lines. Unfortunately, Lloyd was also a chronic alcoholic and Derek resumed drinking in his company.

Kevin played the role of 'Tosh' Lines continuously from 1988 until he was sacked from *The Bill* in 1998 for a lack of punctuality and failing to learn his lines while under the influence of drink. Within days, he was admitted to a clinic for detoxification and was given sedative medication. He then sneaked out of the clinic and went to the local pub. He returned in an intoxicated state, retired to bed, fell asleep and choked on his own vomit, failing to wake due to the toxic mixture of sedatives and alcohol in his bloodstream. He died in May aged just 49.

Michael Elphick was another actor-mate who died prematurely from the ravages of drink. His losing battle with the bottle was very similar to Derek's downfall. Over a 20-year career covering a wide spectrum of comedy and drama, principally in television, Elphick's tough, world-weary face became famous on the small screen. In 1981, he earned critical praise in the title role of *Private Schultz*, a comedy series about a German soldier caught up in a plot to flood Britain with fake five-pound bank notes in World War Two. Derek appeared in several episodes as Jack the Publican. Because they were both drinkers they got on well together.

Elphick himself told me the story that during the shooting of the series (at Elstree, I believe), Derek proposed that they should both go out for a drink at a local pub, both dressed in German uniforms for a lark. The pub turned out to be a favourite watering hole of US airmen from a nearby base. The sudden appearance of two German soldiers caused quite a stir. After a few drinks, Derek provoked an argument with his out of order comments over America's late entry into World War One and World War Two. 'We only just managed to get out of the place without a punch-up,' recalled Elphick with a smile, 'but it was a close call.' After *Private Schultz*, their paths often crossed in various TV productions.

Michael went on to star in further successes, notably as Ken Boon, the motorcycle-riding private detective in the ITV series *Boon*. During his 'Boon-time', he was on the wagon and kept himself fit and lean. But when he resumed drinking in 1988 a doctor gave him a year to live he if continued imbibing, and he managed to stay clear of alcohol for four years. He started drinking again during the long illness of his partner of 34 years, Julia Alexander, who died of cancer in 1996. Thereafter he was freely described in the press as an alcoholic. Nevertheless, he remained in demand and managed to do his business. 'Drink was taking over my life,' he admitted in 1998, 'I've accepted that it's an illness, a disease.'

The last time I saw Michael, in *Gerry's Club*, he was a sad and grotesque figure—bloated, bleary-eyed, and boozed. Long gone was the athletic hero that used to be the teetotal Ken Boon. But he staggered on. In 2001, he landed a prime role in the BBC

BANG OUT OF ORDER!

TV soap *EastEnders*. He was warned about his drinking during working hours. He began slurring and forgetting his lines. The last straw came when he rolled up drunk and disorderly at the British Soap Awards. His six-month contract was not renewed. He collapsed at home and died in September 2002 at the early age of 55. Always a big spender, he had squandered a fortune on drink. His will showed that after all his many debts were paid, only £50,942 remained.

Tom Bell was a preferred drinking-pal of Derek's when they occasionally worked together. Bell's bright progress was also blighted by alcohol abuse—but he managed to overcome the destructive 'disease'. Early in his career he was tipped for the front ranks of stardom alongside Albert Finney and Tom Courtenay but he never quite made it to the very top. His slim, unsmiling visage brought him much work in all three mediums of show business. In 1959, he starred in Alun Owen's play *Progress to the Park*, both on radio and the stage. Alan Brien of the *Sunday Telegraph* hailed Bell as 'a cocky, tough young actor with muscles in his voice as well as on his bones.' Another critic referred to 'his Cherokee profile and face which is expressive even when it's frozen.' Later in his career, he played the chilling Nazi Adolf Eichmann.

His heavy boozing nearly sank his rising progress. After winning critical acclaim for his performance in the 1962 film *The L-Shaped Room* in which he co-starred with Leslie Caron, he attended the British Film Academy awards ceremony at the London Hilton Hotel, where the wine flowed like water. As Prince Philip was ending his president's speech, Bell, well-pissed at this point, dared to shout out: 'Tell us a funny story!'

The Prince ignored the rude interruption and continued his speech. Again Bell called out: 'Come on, then, tell us a funny story!'

This time the Prince turned to Bell and said, 'If you want a funny story, I suggest you engage a professional comic.'

The audience and the British Film establishment were mortified by the improper incident. Leslie Caron apologised to everyone on Bell's behalf, explaining that 'Tom was a little merry.' The drunken episode brought a definite stall to his promising career but it did not destroy it. He gained the reputation of being a 'naughty boy' when in his cups but (like Derek) nevertheless proved himself to be a solid actor, delivering numerous brilliant performances on stage, television, and in films. Born in Liverpool in 1933, the same year as Derek, they worked together in several TV productions, including the series *Reilly Ace of Spies*, and in the BBC film *Seconds Out*, in which Derek played a boxing manager. The screenplay was written by Lynda La Plante, who had been at RADA with Derek. Tom Bell continued working almost to the end of his life, having given up alcohol for the last 15 years. He died in 2006 aged 73.

In July 1998 death claimed Johnny Speight, Derek's old sparring partner in early comedy writing. He was 78. Johnny had enjoyed a long run of national success lasting some 30 years. He created that great television anti-hero Alf Garnett, the loud-mouthed Cockney bigot of the popular series *Till Death Us Do Part*, played with such gusto by Warren Mitchell. With the ascendancy of political correctness, Speight's blunt and vernacular style of satire went out of fashion and his later projects were not developed by over-cautious TV companies. Derek and

Johnny were long-time friends and show business colleagues.

Seven days after Johnny's demise, the Grim Reaper snatched the life of the lovely Leena Skoog, Derek's lover during his tour of *Darling Mr London* in 1975. A Swedish fashion model, singer and actress, Leena travelled the world. On her return to Sweden, she switched careers and became a teacher. The delightful Leena, so full of fun and vitality, died of cancer at only 47. A month later Derek would take his final curtain and exit his last painful performance of life.

*****

During his last few years, Derek fought a seesaw battle with alcohol, and lost every punishing round. On the booze and off the booze, he was now a boring old has-been. He was in and out of the hospital constantly. On one occasion, his local GP refused to help him: 'How dare you come to my surgery drunk... Get out!'

His physical condition had so deteriorated, especially his right knee, that he was forced to use a pair of crutches. He had been medically advised to have the leg amputated. Every time we spoke on the phone he had a tale of woe; he would mumble away with long, Pinteresque pauses, not making much sense. I feared for his mental health.

He told me in some sorry detail about the sad little sequence that involved a painful visit to the local office of the Inland Revenue. He hobbled there on crutches. It started to rain and he got soaking wet. As he made his crippled way, step by cautious step, he concentrated his rheumy gaze on the pavement, anxious not to slip on the wet leaves underfoot, knowing that if he fell he would injure himself even further and not be able to get upright by his own efforts.

Sitting in the tax office like a sodden tramp, he pleaded his case of non-payment: 'I have no money. I can't work and I can't pay the tax you demand. I don't know what to do... I'm at my wits end...' Then, in a final burst of frustrated defiance—'And to be honest, I don't give a monkey's fuck what you do... You can't get blood out of a stone!' End of interview, and he stomped out into the rain.

Derek himself must have come to an earlier conclusion that he had nothing more to give to his chosen profession. And without the focus, the self-discipline demanded by the acting process, he must have recognised the inevitable truth that he had no reason to continue the struggle. So bring down the final curtain: 'Farewell and fuck 'em all... I have nothing left to give.'

He surrendered what remained of his life to vodka. A bottle a day kept reality at bay; two bottles a day brought oblivion. Shabnam found him very ill in the flat, unable to move, an empty bottle of vodka by his side. An ambulance rushed him to the Charing Cross Hospital in Hammersmith. The doctors could not save him, he was too far gone. He fell into a coma and died on 11 August 1998 aged 65 years and two months.

I saw him last, face to face, on his deathbed a few days before the end. His eyes were closed. I perceived a faint look of fixed contempt on his yellowish, immobile visage... defiant to the last. When I saw his Death Certificate I noted that, officially, he had triumphed in our old argument about disease versus addiction. Cause of death: a) Liver failure b) Alcoholic Liver Disease. His two sons scattered his ashes into the Thames directly outside the National Theatre, venue of his greatest performances, after which we held a jovial family memorial lunch in the Mezzanine Restaurant in the main building.

There followed a sad but convivial gathering of actors and staff in the NT's Ashcroft Room, in which a giant-sized colour image of Derek dominated one end of the crowded chamber; he was dressed in the 16th-century costume of the Spanish soldier Rebolledo in Pedro Calderon de la Barca's *The Mayor of Zalamea* (staged at the Cottesloe in 1981). The muster included Paul Scofield, Harold Pinter, Bill Bryden, Sebastian Graham-Jones, Michael Gough, Tony Haygarth, Trevor Ray, and other surviving members of the Cottesloe Company. All spoke highly and amusingly of Derek's notable ability, his loyalty, his comradeship, and yes, his often excessive behaviour.

The Guardian newspaper of 15 August 1998 published an obituary by Keith Dewhurst, the playwright, who had known Derek very well over the years:

A SOLDIER ON THE STAGE
To begin with the bad side. Derek Newark, who has died aged 65, was a joke to some people, and caused offence to many more—as often as not those with power and no real talent... Newark began his adult life in the Coldstream Guards [and] in his heart's core he was forever a soldier...

It was as a crucial member of Bill Bryden's National Theatre [Cottesloe] troupe in the late 1970s and early 1980s that he appeared in [many productions]... In those days of Peter Hall's enlightened NT actors appeared for all the directors in all [three] arenas and Derek had comic triumphs in a revival of *Plunder* by Ben Travers and Alan Ayckbourn's *Bedroom Farce*, and extraordinary platform performances of Kipling, the Putney Debates, and impersonating WC Fields. He also took time out to be in Harold Pinter's *The Hothouse* at Hampstead—a role that perhaps gave the clue to his value.

Derek was trouble already: vodkas and tonic, macho metaphors, abuse in the Green Room of fellow actors who he considered had 'lost their bottle'. But Pinter, like every proper director who worked with Derek, and every writer, was no fool. He knew that when the first night came, and the atmosphere was against you, there was one person who never lost his bottle—England's actor, the soldier who fought to the last man... on the stage he had unshakeable calm. He acted the play properly. There were no cheap tricks... that is why Pinter picked him—and why I, who wrote four television and six stage plays in which he appeared, would put him down first on every team sheet. Not a great wasted star, but a hero nonetheless, who parlayed for the audience an entire theatrical dream. When the dream fizzled out, Derek went with it...

Four days later, *The Guardian* published the following obituary letter from Harold Pinter:

It was a great shock to read of the death of Derek Newark. I worked with him twice. He played Ajax in *The Trojan War Will not Take Place* at the National [Theatre] and Roote in my play *The Hothouse* in the theatre and on television. He was a great comic actor. I have never laughed so much in my life as I did at the first reading of *The Hothouse* at Hampstead [Theatre] when his outraged exasperation with the crassness of those around him assumed monumental proportions... Off-stage he could certainly be pretty rumbustious— 'out of order'—as he himself would put it, but he was at core a gentle and generous man. I treasure his memory.

Derek's eldest son Quentin, a graphic designer, created a small photographic memorial booklet on his father's life and times and sent copies to Derek's friends and colleagues at home and abroad. Jean, his loyal wife of thirty years, received many letters of condolence. I select just a few to demonstrate the affection and admiration that Derek acquired during his long acting career. From Richard Mangan, the then Adminstrator of the Mander & Mitchensen Theatre Collection:

Dear Jean,
I was very, very sorry to hear the sad news of Derek's death. I worked with him at the National and he was kind enough to take part in the Platform Performance of Kipling's *Barrackroom Ballads* which I put together. Whatever Derek's shortcomings, I have to say that I can think of no-one who made me laugh quite as much

as he did—there were many evenings when I, and many others, were simply helpless with mirth. He was a fine actor, a good friend for many years and he will be greatly missed... I shall remember him in my prayers.

From Brian Cox, Scottish stage actor and international film star, who had known Derek since the Cottesloe years:

Dear Jean,
I can't tell you how sad I was to hear about Derek. As irascible as he was, I loved him dearly and what a talent—what a great talent. The booklet I received—here in New York where I am doing *Art* on Broadway—what a wonderful testament it is, imaginative and succinct. It was prepared with great tenderness. My love and condolences to you and your family.

From Frederick Treves, veteran actor of stage and screen and National Theatre colleague:

Dear Jean,
I am deeply touched that you sent me your son's booklet on Derek's life. We were not close friends, but I did admire enormously his considerable talents as a fine actor and for his off-stage wit, and his considerable charm and understanding of those of us who were of a lesser talent.

I worked with him at the NT in *The Iceman Cometh* in 1980 [Treves played Cecil Lewis, one-time captain of

BANG OUT OF ORDER!

British infantry; Derek was Ed Moser, one-time circus man]. He was quite brilliant. I remember him so well in *Bedroom Farce* with dear Brenda Blethyn. I also recall his superb performance in *Glengarry Glen Ross*.

I also remember well the party at Purley [Derek and Jean's home] in the garden on a fine summer day, when all the close team of Bill Bryden's 'Rugby Club' were there: Jack Shepherd, Gawn Grainger, and many of his dearest friends. It was a very memorable, happy day...

Julia MacDermot, Derek's agent for many years, concurred that he could indeed be very funny, and very contentious at times.

His wit was legendary. He could take the most mundane word or remark and transform it into a hilarious and seemingly logical half-hour fantasy. But he could be maddening. One Sunday evening I had gone to bed with a streaming cold. At 10 o'clock the phone rang. It was Derek. 'Julia, are you my bloody agent or not? What have you done with my bloody insurance card?' Spitting with fury, I told him what to do with his insurance card, and if he ever did this again he wouldn't have a bloody agent. There was a little pause, and then, in a kindly voice, as if explaining something to a dim-witted idiot, he said, 'Oh, come along love, let's face it, at your age, without me to rattle you up, you'd be a basket case.' There was no answer to that!

The last years were not happy. One could use the old cliché 'He was his own worst enemy'—but Derek was no cliché, he was a 'one-off'. Perhaps he was striving for something, took a wrong turning and lost his way. Those close to him caught glimpses of extreme vulnerability and, when it came to the crunch, great kindness. The business has lost a big talent and I have lost a loyal client and friend who made me laugh more than anyone I have ever met. I quote from Alan Ayckbourn: 'Derek's *Spotlight* entry should read, DEREK NEWARK—EVERY AGENT SHOULD HAVE ONE.'

It's no use postulating what I might have been... I am the things I have done and nothing more.

Jean-Paul Sartre

Index

Agutter, Derek 43, 76
Anderson, Lindsay 66, 184
Andrews, Harry 66, 155-156
Ashcroft, Peggy 16
Attenborough, Richard 82-83, 159-160
Aukin, David 149, 151, 152
Ayckbourn, Alan 136-137, 139, 140, 244, 248

Baby Elephant, The 90-92
Bacon, Francis 197-206
Barlow 103-104, 128
Bedroom Farce 122, 136-137, 138-146, 153, 160, 244, 247
Belcher, Muriel 195, 199-200
Bell, Tom 239-240
Bellman and True 125, 184-185, 219
Bindon, John 10-15
Blethyn, Brenda 135, 247
Blue Max, The 70-71, 72, 74, 76, 77, 78, 79, 120
Board, Ian 195, 200-201

Bogarde, Dirk 158
Brando, Marlon 213
Brecht, Bertolt 62, 90-94
Brittain, Sergeant Major Ronald 33-35, 117
Bryden, Bill 88, 89-92, 107, 109-111, 112, 114, 130, 160, 162, 166, 172-175, 176, 181-182, 183-184, 216, 227, 232, 243, 247
Budgie 96, 99-100, 120

Callow, Simon 114
Carter, Jim 112, 113, 166, 184
Churchill, Winston 190-191
Cinderella 176-178, 232
Connery, Sean 99
Coward, Noel 142-143, 158, 236
Cox, Brian 112, 246
Cranham, Kenneth 88, 112, 131, 169, 171

Darling Mr London 105-106

Dewhurst, Keith 39, 70, 88, 89, 111, 112, 127, 148, 160, 243-244
Diamond, Lew 24-25
Dillon, Michael 206
Dispatches 148
Doctor Who 65-66, 95, 113, 234
Durkin, Patrick 217-218
Dyer, George 202-206

Elphick, Michael 153, 237-239
End of Conflict 60-62, 64, 119, 188

Faith, Adam 96, 99-100, 120
Farson, Daniel 197-198
Fernald, John 48-53
Fields, W C 169-170, 244
Finlay, Frank 16, 135
Finney, Albert 144, 166, 239
Flynn, Jeremy 181
Fox, Edward 64-65, 82
Fraser, Ronald 234

Gielgud, John 9, 82, 110, 154-158, 178, 232
Glengarry Glen Ross 124, 171-175, 184, 247
Glover, Brian 88, 112, 235-236
Golden Boy 125, 180-182
Gough, Michael 109, 111, 136, 139, 142-144, 243

Grade, Michael 193
Grainger, Gawn 112, 247
Grantham, Leslie 187-189
Griffith, Hugh 62
Groucho Letters, The 121, 132-134

Hall, Peter 84, 107, 111, 114, 129, 137, 138, 140, 148, 209, 227, 244
Hall, Willis 60, 98
Harvey, Laurence 232-233
Haygarth, Tony 160, 161, 164-165, 177, 243
Hickson, Joan 136, 138, 139, 142, 144
Hill, Bernard 184, 219
Hiller, Wendy 185
Hochhuth, Rolf 190-191, 220
Hoskins, Bob 11, 88, 94, 112, 167, 179
Hothouse, The 9, 11, 148-152, 158-159, 244-245
Huggett, Richard 134

Il Campiello 109-111, 128

Jacobi, Derek 54, 154
Jarvis, Martin 53, 168, 169
Jason, David 105, 106
Jerome, Roger 53, 63
Johns, Stratford 103-104

Johnson, Karl 112, 173
Judd, Edward 56-58

Keith, Penelope 54
Kingsley, Ben 159, 160
Kossoff, David 25
Kray Twins 10, 188, 202

Landen, Dinsdale 16, 135
Lansbury, Angela 141
Lasch, Ronnie 22-24
Last Decathlon 179-180
Leaney, Fred 23-24
Lemmon, Jack 175
Loach, Ken 12, 236
Lloyd, Kevin 228, 237
Littler, Susan 136, 138, 139, 140, 144

MacDermot, Julia 84, 247-248
Madoc, Philip 102
Mamet, David 171-175
Mangan, Richard 131, 245-246
Margaret, Princess 135, 161-163, 178
Marx, Groucho 131-134
Massey, Daniel 63, 95, 118, 154, 236
McCoy, Sylvester 113
McKellen, Ian 60-61
McManus, Mark 88, 127, 183, 231
Metcalf, Lennie 145-146

Midsummer Night's Dream, A 160-163
Miller, Arthur 15, 189
Mitchell, Bill 234-235
Mysteries, The 113, 183-184

Nesbitt, Derren 70, 76-77, 81-82, 186, 194
Newark, Elle Marie 19
Newark, George Kenneth 19, 214
Newark, George William 19-20, 88
Newark, Jean, nee Thornhill 44-45, 47, 106, 165-166, 211-212, 218-219, 245-247
Newark, Quentin 211, 245
Newark, Tim 167
Nichols, Dandy 16
Norman, Frank 196-197

Oh! What a Lovely War 65, 82-83, 96, 159
Olivier, Laurence 107, 109, 110, 155, 178, 190, 232-233
O'Toole, Peter 153

Peppard, George 70-76
Pertwee, Jon 95, 214, 234
Pinter, Harold 9, 60, 112, 148-152, 158-159, 167-169, 172-173, 244-245

Pirates 89-90
Plunder 134-136, 244

Quick, Diana 16
Quilley, Denis 16

RADA 47-55, 63, 76, 87, 102, 105, 227
Ratcliffe, Ian 207-209
Reed, Oliver 66, 68-69
Richardson, Ralph 16, 82
Rigby, Terence 53, 63
Rising Damp 104
Robinson, Doug 99, 102
Robinson, Elizabeth 56, 65, 84
Robinson, Joe 99

Scofield, Paul 84, 101, 110, 160, 161, 163, 232, 243
Shadroui, Richard 146-147
Sharpe, Bernard 179, 180
Shepherd, Jack 39-40, 88, 111, 112, 127, 161, 162-163, 173-175, 176-177, 181-182, 184, 247
Skoog, Leena 106, 240
Smith, Maggie 16, 82, 232
Soldiers 190-191
Speight, Johnny 25-28, 186, 240
Staircase 84-85, 101
Steiger, Rod 170

Stephens, Robert 112, 163, 176-177, 231-234

Thorn in the Flesh, The 80-81
Timothy, Christopher 170
Travers, Ben 51, 118, 135-136, 244
Treves, Frederick 246-247

Ward, Simon 141, 185
Waterhouse, Keith 60, 221
White, Arthur 105
Winstone, Ray 113, 224-226
Williams, Tennessee 141
Winner, Michael 66-69, 186, 192-194